2 Good 2 Be 4 Gotten

Ozarks Folklore and Culture during the Twentieth Century and Before

By

Max Decker, Ed. D.

©2012 by Max Decker, Ed. D.
All rights reserved
Printed in the United States of America

ISBN 978-1-105-96905-8

Dedicated to my Wife, Mona
and to our Daughter, Becky

Contents

Acknowledgments xi
Foreword xiii
Introduction 1

Chapter 1   The Setting, the Country, the People 9

Chapter 2   Mysterious Places and Events 13
                   Sweetin Pond 14
                   Taylor's Cave 15
                   The Horse Thief 17
                   The "Blue Man" or "Wild Man"
                   Of the Ozarks 20

Chapter 3   Ozark Individuals 25
                   Depression Time in the Ozarks 26
                   Peddlers 34
                   Drummers 36
                   Tramps 37
                   Outlaws 37
                   Preachers 38
                   Candidates for Office 42
                   Granny-Women 45
                   Ozark Mountain Doctors and
                   Dentist 45

Chapter 4   Childlore 55
                   Autograph Verses 55
                   A Play with Words 57
                   A Wish 59
                   Love 59
                   Marriage 62
                   Courtship 63
                   Yours Till 64

Chapter 4 (cont.)

Advice 64
Wondering What to Write 65
Remember Me 65
Writer's Situation 66
Friendship 66

Games 66
   Slap Hands 67
   Shinny 67
   Hide the Thimble 68
   Drop the Handkerchief 68
   Stink Base 68
   Hull Gull 69
   Horn Horn 69
   Sheep in My Pen 70
   Bluffman 70
   Pig in My Pen 70
   Wolf Over the Ridge 71
   Two Deep 71
   Tag 71
   Wood Tag 72
   Ante-Over 72
   New Orleans 72
   Wave 73
   Spin the Bottle 73
   Mother, May I 73
   Pleased or Displeased 74
   Red Rover 74
   Tap the Rabbit 74
   Goul Down 75
   Rounder 76
   Board on Deck 76
   Geography Match 77
   Cipher 78

	Fox and Geese 79
	King of the Mountain 79
	Red Line 79
	Fruit Basket 79
	Laugh and Go Foot 80
	Bluejay 80
	Tumblebug Wager 80
	The Snake Game 81
	The Doodlebug Game 81
	Stick Horses 82
	Horseshoes 82
	Marbles 82
	Choosing Up 90
Chapter 5	**Folksay** 91
	Sayings 91
	Bywords 97
	Mispronunciations 99
	Comparisons 99
	Conversation 102
	Place Names 104
	Local Journalism 109
Chapter 6	**Epitaphs** 113
Chapter 7	**Remedies** 123
Chapter 8	**Times for Planting** 133
Chapter 9	**Signs of the Weather** 143
	Rain 144
	Bad Weather 145
	Good Weather 146
	Snow and Cold 146
	Good and Bad Weather 146
	A Change in the Weather 147

	Frost	147
	Miscellaneous	147
Chapter 10	**Entertainment**	**151**
	The Pie Supper	152
	Picnics	156
	Cake Suppers	162
	Play Parties	163
	Music Parties	163
	Songs, Singing and Other Country Music	166
	Reading Material	169
	Tricksters	177
	Jokes and Short Stories	187
	Telephone Entertainment	201
	Dancing	205
	Weddings and Charivaris	208
	Photography	211
	Kangaroo Court	213
	Fun with Anvils, Cotton Rocks And Shot Guns	215
	Memorial Day or Decoration Day	216
	To Course a Bee	217
Chapter 11	**Farm Customs**	**219**
	Butchering	224
	Threshing	226
	Molasses Making	228
Chapter 12	**Church Activities**	**231**
	All-Day Meeting and Dinner-On-the-Ground	232
	Church Business Meetings	236
	The Church Debate	238
	Baptizings	239

	Protracted Meetings	241
	The Brush Arbor	242
Chapter 13	**A Death in the Family**	**247**
Chapter 14	**One-room Schools in the Ozarks**	**253**
Chapter 15	**Folk History**	**271**
	Murders	271
	Tall Tales	273
	A Tale of Buck on Bald Knob Mountain	274
	A Tale of the Three Who Went West	275
	Horns and a Dilemma	276
Chapter 16	**The Supernatural**	**281**
	Beliefs	282
	Ghost Stories	285
	The Ghost at Rocky Crossin'	286
	The Old Haint	288
	Ghost or No Ghost	289
	The Haunted House	289
	The Singing Kettle	290
	Rappin's	290
	The Haunted House by a Headless Ghost	291
	Rail Fence Ghost	293
	The Church Place Ghost	294
	The Man-Eating Booger of Booger County	295
	Telling Your Fortune	297
	Marked Babies	298
Endnotes		301
Sources, Notes and Information		303

Acknowledgments

I want to express my appreciation to Dr. John Brewton, who was chairperson of the Department of English at George Peabody College of Vanderbilt University and who was my major advisor when I studied folklore there. He guided me and encouraged me through much of the research for an independent study on Ozark Folklore.

I want to thank Dr. Gordon McCann of Springfield, Missouri, for his encouragement, advice and interest in my writing. Dr. McCann co-authored *Ozark Folklore, A Bibliography* with Vance Randolph, Vol. II, University of Missouri Press, 1987.

Dr. W.K. McNeil, folklorist at the Ozark Folk Center, Mtn. View, Arkansas, gave me valuable advice during my research of Ozark Folklore.

I want to extend my appreciation to the typist/editor, Marie Dickison Bristol and the illustrator, Jean Lirley Huff.

Also, thank you to Cinita and Logan Brown for their encouragement over the years.

Foreword

The misconception that many people have of Ozark hill people needs to be laid to rest. We are not the type that some movie makers have tried to portray. We are not the image that some people in urban America have of us. We are not ignorant, backward, shy, dirty or dirt poor. We have our share of people with problems but not any more than any other area of the country.

Our environment and inherited traits have combined to make us highly intelligent people. From our midst have come people recognized over the world: educators, lawyers, national legislators, ministers, writers, artists, astronauts, actors and actresses, playwrights, musicians, farmers and common people who believed and still believe that hard work is honorable.

And, our environment and our inherited traits have combined to make us a highly adaptable people who, as you will read in this book, were creative, who endured hardships but entertained themselves, who had a work ethic like no other people in the world and who laughed and cried but made a respectable place for their families in this world.

We are not Easterners, Westerners, Southerners, or Northerners. We are people from the Ozarks Mountains. But we respect others and their cultural heritage and often wish that they would respect ours.

2 Good
2 Be
———
4 Gotten

Introduction

Folklore and culture of the Ozark Mountains was selected as the subject of this book in order that some of the unwritten lore and customs of the region, which has been a part of the traditions of the people since the early settlements, may be preserved and studied as a factor in the growth and development of this mountain country, and so that a direct contribution may be made to the literature of America.

Although there has been some investigation of the folklore and culture of the Ozarks which has been published in several good books, it was the purpose of this writer to gather material directly from the people. No reliance was made on published material, except for a few quotes from newspapers and favorite books that they loved to read for entertainment.

An attempt has been made to gather material of the following classifications: mysterious places and events, Ozark individuals, childlore, folksay, epitaphs, remedies, times for planting, signs of the weather, entertainment, farm customs, church activities, death and burial customs, one-room rural schools, folk history and the supernatural.

Mysterious places and events include unusual stories that were exciting to people years ago and are still talked about today.

Ozark individuals include stories of how people managed to survive during the Depression, peddlers, drummers, tramps, outlaws, preachers, candidates for office, granny-women and country doctors and dentists.

Childlore covers such things as games played by children at home and at the one-room school and autograph verses they wrote.

Folksay includes sayings, bywords, mispronunciations, comparisons, conversation, place names and local journalism.

Epitaphs is a chapter by itself since it stands alone as an acknowledgment of the life of a loved one who has died.

Remedies were included since they were a very important factor in the existence of the people since many lived a long distance from a doctor or hospital.

Times for planting were important to the people because if they did not grow enough food, they would go hungry.

Signs of the weather gave hill people an idea of what to expect when they decided to plant a crop, harvest or entertain themselves.

Entertainment was a major part of the life of these hill people. If they could look forward to a week-end of enjoyment, they felt more like working during the week. Entertainment included such events as pie suppers, picnics, cake suppers, play parties, music parties, songs and fiddle and dance tunes, reading material, tricksters, jokes and short stories, the telephone, dancing, weddings and charivaries, photography, Kangaroo court, fun with anvils, cotton rocks and shot guns, Memorial Day activities and to course a bee.

Farm customs included butchering, thrashing and molasses making.

Church activities were important because many were highly religious and the church house was the center of community activity. Church activities included all-day-meetings and dinner-on-the-ground, church business meetings, church debates, baptizings, protracted meetings and the brush arbor.

A death in the family was treated as a sacred event. People respected their dead.

The one-room school was the center of many local activities.

Folk history includes accounts of murders and tall tales. Few people ever forgot murders and tall tales.

The supernatural played an important part in the lives of these people. Beliefs, including water witching, ghost stories, fortune telling and marked babies were entertaining to talk about.

The Great Depression had a great impact on these hill people. What they did to survive and what they had and did not have is unbelievable to many people today.

Many people liked to tell hunting stories. Some of them were true and some of them may have been exaggerations. But they were important and relevant because this was one way of survival.

A wide sampling of the Ozark population was made. Older people were the primary source because they seemed to have more authentic stories of the days "way back there." Much information was obtained from local historians, country doctors, fox hunters, country storekeepers, my parents and my grandparents.

However two major sources gave me much of my material. The first source was my grandmother, Tennessee James Martin, (1860-1941), who lived with us until I was eleven years old. She sang songs to me; she told me many stories; played games with me and gave me plenty of remedies that helped me to survive. The second source is the period of time I have lived in the Ozarks, 1929 to the present. This time was filled with much of the lore and customs that I will tell in this book. So I have enjoyed a first hand experience. I have lived in the "backwoods." I have enjoyed the spine tingling ghost stories since I was a small boy. I have seen, smelled and tasted the beautiful colored pills in the country doctor's pill bag. I have felt the sorrow of death and burial of Ozark people. I have smelled "store boughten" bread. I have seen lice on peoples' heads. I have tasted corn liquor. I have seen my mother and grandmother make soap and hominy in the open kettle. I have attended and taught in a one-room country school. And I have run from the itch. I am a person who knows and respects his people. I am one of them.

It is hoped that the material in this book will in some small way contribute to a better understanding of Ozark Mountain people--what caused them to laugh, to cry and react in different ways.

Yet, any writer, even one who writes of an investigation of this type, must give the facts, the bitter and the sweet, the beautiful and the ugly, because this is true life and folklore and culture must be from the mouths of the people who developed it, who practiced it, and who believed it.

From the southern Appalachian Mountains they came in their wagons and on horseback. They crossed rich farm land in the Mississippi Delta and came to a region much like the one they had left. They were looking for a good spring of water and plenty of game to kill and eat. And they found what they wanted in the Ozarks. To be a mountain man was nothing new. To have the strength and determination to survive in a rugged land was part of their heritage.

An incident a few years ago proves that the people still have the will to withstand whatever may get in their way.

They may be superstitious about the causes and the results but they have learned to meet whatever challenges them. They have learned to take life as it comes, to endure the evils of their environment but to not forsake their ability to survive. They know that these are their responsibilities to themselves, their families and their community.

The incident was as follows: It was late in August. The weather was scorching hot with little wind. From sunup to sunset there was no relief. And even at night the intense heat seemed to creep in and seek refuge. Dust was everywhere. It covered the scrub oak along the roads and the green grass was burned black. Even the houses and barns had a film of light brown dirt. Now and then a gust of the dry powder was picked up and swept in every direction by fierce yet small whirlwinds. One could track themselves in it.

Katydids and tree frogs creaked and croaked lazily for they had had a dreary summer of work.

The sky was a bird-egg blue color with only a few small fluffy clouds miles away which looked to be stationary designs against the far away blue.

The grass in the fields was burned black and brown with only a hint of burned green here and there.

The corn crop looked sick. Its leaves had curled at first then turned black and crisp.

Cattle and horses strolled slowly along the shady places near the small seep holes of water which would not last long. There was a thick film of dust and dirt on their backs.

The only things that seemed to be free from the heat were the buzzards that sailed high in the sky looking for whatever they could find. Frequently, they could be seen sailing down for they had found a starved-to-death victim.

Day after day the temperature reached well above one-hundred degrees and dropped only into the nineties at night.

After several weeks of this trying weather, thunder clouds appeared on different occasions, far-away thunder could be heard, faint streaks of lightning appeared but they soon vanished in the sky and the heat became even worse.

At different times there was other hope. One morning the sun rose dripping gold and everyone said "red in the morning, shepherd's warning." They just knew there would be rain within twenty-four hours. But no rains came.

Cows were seen carrying dried grass in the corners of their mouths and everyone gave a sigh of relief, for now, for sure, the drought would break. But there was no relief.

On several mornings rocks could be seen sweating, even dripping with water, it seemed, but no one saw any rain. A number of people said their bones ached. Whip-poor-wills called during the day; squirrels stirred at high noon and a star moved near the moon but no signs seemed to work. Still no rains came.

The conditions grew worse by the hour. Springs went dry. Seep holes were now only crusts of dried dirt. Farmers soon began to haul water from the rivers, which were low, for their stock. But they knew they could not do this for long. They would have to sell, and in a few days this is what they began to do. People waited in long lines of trucks for their turn to unload their shrinking cattle at the stockyard chutes; soon prices dropped more, to almost nothing. Farmers took a big loss not only in price per hundred but also in shrinkage. But still they had to go to market. The trucks moved on.

The severe conditions continued through September and into October. Fall rains were sure to come soon, everyone thought.

The leaves of the trees began to show their fall change of color, but it was not the pretty bright red-orange, red and rich brown; it was a sad light brown from lack of moisture.

Everyone had just about given up hope that there would ever be any relief. People became frustrated to the point that they were antagonistic with one another. What was there to make them happy? Little hay was made. The corn was only about one-third of a crop. The fall pastures were nothing that could be eaten and there was no profit from the cattle. There was no wonder they were irritable. No rain! No rain! No rain!

"I've never seen anything like it in sixty years. We've not had anything like this since the 1800's. Beats all I've ever seen. All signs have failed—signs that have worked all my life. Now that I am an old man they have disappointed me. But that star, that one that has moved close to the moon again. Can't keep thinking something will come from it," an elderly man said.

One night several weeks later everyone went to bed as usual in the heat. However, at about one o'clock in the morning they were awakened by a roar of thunder and long streaks of lightning flashing across the sky. When they went out to see what was taking place, they saw rain and the dark clouds. They saw not just thunder clouds far in the distance but great billows of dark clouds going in every direction, mixing, as some said, in the sky. The thunder continued to roar. The lightning continued to flash. And, the rains came. Three inches came that night.

When people arose the next morning, they looked out on a different world, a cleaner brighter world. Even the dead grass in the fields seemed to take on a slightly greener cast. "Thank goodness we got some relief," they said.

"It was that star that moved close to the moon," said the

old man. Another said it was providence. But whatever it was, more rains came. Torrents of water just ran down from the sky as the clouds seemed to burst above.

The dust had become a mess of mud everywhere. Cars became stuck along the roads and what livestock that had been saved and not sold made deep tracks in the fields.

Two days passed and the rains came again, heavy. Farmers began to wish they had not sold their cattle.

For three weeks rains drenched the once hot and dirty earth and at frequent intervals "gully washers" washed the dried ground. Ponds over-flowed; creeks climbed out of their banks and washed fences away.

The rains had provided enough water, in fact, too much. They could stop anytime. Fall seeding needed to be done but the rains came on. By this time people had forgotten much of the dust and heat that they had endured so long. But now they were faced with a new problem. Yet they must live on. They knew that they must endure as they had before. They knew that they must realize that nature is cruel at times, that it waits for no one, gives to no one, respects no one. They knew that they must always be ready to face the dust and the rains.

This one example illustrates how people of the Ozarks are ready to face their problems. Bolstered by their way of life, their region and their faith in God, they are well aware of who they are, what they have and are thankful for it.

Chapter 1

The Setting, the Country, the People

The Ozark Mountains, Ozark Plateau or Ozark Hills, call them what you like, stretch from the southern part of Illinois across south central and southwest Missouri into north central and northwest Arkansas into a small part of southeast Kansas and into eastern Oklahoma. The land is rough and hilly. Yet in the valleys and along the rivers is some of the most fertile soil in the States. The hills are covered with a dense growth of oak, cedar, pine and many other species of trees.

This area is infested with a breed of animals known to most people as hillbillies. To many people such a person is long and lean with a good crop of whiskers; they believe they go barefooted all the time and that the only labor they do is toting a jug of moonshine over their arm. They think of this hill man as a person who lacks intellect and appreciation for culture. Of course, this is not a true picture, but people are not bothered by the description.

"If I didn't have more to worry about than that, I would be in good shape," they would reply.

Most people in the Ozarks and many tourists agree that this is a beautiful region but the tourists cannot understand how we turn the rocks and hills into enough cornbread and molasses on which to survive.

The majority of the towns are small yet they are pleasant places to visit and provide a wonderful setting for the legends and tales that are still a part of the lives of the people.

However, some of the settlements, as is the case in every region, are less desirable. In one town a few years ago a man was seen driving down a stake in a courthouse lawn of a small county seat. Several people gathered around and asked him what on earth he was doing.

"My pa told me iffin I ever found hell right here on earth, to drive down a stake to warn the next feller. And by damn that is just what I'm adoin'."[1]

Another man who was driving from one town to another noticed the population sign at the edge of town. It read: "Population--nine hundred seventy-five. Nine hundred-fifty good citizens and twenty-five damn fools."[2] So one can understand that there are a few of us who cannot see all the good all the time.

Most people in the Ozarks are known for their honesty. A drummer traveling in southern Missouri and northern Arkansas got the idea that most people trusted the neighbors. One day he came to a country store and post office. The front door was locked. No one was around. But he saw a sign tacked on the front door. The sign had been placed above a small hole in the door. The sign read, CROP TIME HAS CAME. I HAVE GONE TO THE FIELD. MAIL DAYS ARE MONDAYS, WEDNESDAYS AND SATURDAYS. IF YOU OWE ME ANYTHING, JUST POKE IT IN THE HOLE.

I was talking to a man who lived near a small town in the Ozarks. It was a nice town and had attracted several people from the North. They had bought homes and moved from the city.

"Yeah, they come here and try to tell us what's wrong and how to do everything their way. They stay about two years and go back North to the city were they came from. But, by golly while they were here, we got most of their money."

Bob Holt, a native Ozarker, who lives in Douglas County near Ava, Missouri, is a rancher and one of the best fiddle players in the Ozarks. He says his description of the people is that they are honest, will, for the most part, keep their word, are hard workers and clean. Bob says that they may not have fancy clothes and those they have may have a patch now and then but they are clean.

The majority of the early settlers of this region migrated from the states of Tennessee, Kentucky, North and South Carolina and Virginia. They brought with them the legends and the lore, the songs and tales which were mostly of English background. From the frontier grew more superstitions, tall tales and strange customs. Many of these types of lore have faded away with our "so called" modern age but many remain in the hearts and minds of the people. However, much of the lore and culture of the past is being lost every day as people who loved and preserved and practiced it pass on. This is why it is so important to search, record and preserve the past of the Ozarks.

Many of the legends, songs, tall tales, and customs have different versions. One can hear a tall tale in one section of the Ozarks and hear the same tale told in a much different way in another section.

For example, the song "Barbara Allen" has been sung in the Ozarks for many years but there are about as many ways to sing the song as there are people. And today most people of "true blood" will argue that the words to their version are the correct ones and only ones.

Yet what is more important in the study of this region is the fact that the cultural heritage of the people has a solid foundation which came from one mountain region to another.

Many people have had the foresight and the wisdom to preserve some of the lore and culture. Some have written books. Many have recorded songs. But some people in Arkansas had an idea that preserved much of what we are. The Ozark Folk Center near Mtn. View, Arkansas, is a center of Ozark lore and cultural preservation.

There one can travel back to the time of their ancestors and enjoy and understand what they did to survive and entertain themselves. Music copyrighted before 1941 played on all types of mountain musical instruments such as the fiddle and banjo can be heard every day from April through October. One can view the herbal gardens, basket weaving, soap making, molasses making, spinning, weaving, quilt making, blacksmithing, printing, candle making, furniture making and many other things our ancestors did.

Music, singing and dancing is enjoyed by the staff and the visitors. The two-step, waltz, jig and square dance is done like it was done one hundred years ago.

Those who are responsible for this preservation center and the State of Arkansas must be commended for saving some of the culture of the Ozarks. It is, indeed, too good to be forgotten.

Chapter 2

Mysterious Places and Events

Every community has its town characters, interesting places or strange events. And what is so interesting is not so much the story of the person or the event but the number of years it has been told, the manner in which it was told and the belief that so many people have in it. One would not think that a man or woman who swore and used dirty language all their life, who treated their neighbors with scorn, and was hated by most everyone who knew them would live in the minds of the people for years, but they do. And again, one would not think that many people would believe in stories of buried treasures, but they do. One would not think of people laughing and telling stories about the terrible treatment of local preachers in some communities, but they seem to enjoy it.

Many of the mysterious places where buried treasures are supposed to be buried have already been researched and recorded. This area of mysterious places has been researched well by other authors and collectors and there were not many of them to begin with. It is like Pop Ramsey of Mtn. View, Arkansas told me when I asked him about buried treasures in that part of the Ozarks.

"Nobody back then had anything much of value to bury," he said.

Pop did say that a man at church one day said he was about six inches from a slab of silver.

"If that had been me, I wouldn't have been talking about it. I would have been out there diggin'," Pop said.

Sweetin Pond

Everyone who lives in or near the community of Dora, Missouri, knows some type of story about the mysterious Sweetin Pond, a large lake-like pond near this small place. It is noted for its large fish, muddy water and mysterious depth. It is said that for many years people have caught large carp fish in the deep waters. Years ago the water was muddy at times, yet at other times, for no reason, the water became blue and clear.

Many attempts have been made to measure the depth. My grandfather and several of his friends tied anvils to hundreds of feet of rope and let it down. But they never reached the bottom.

They dumped bundles of straw and sacks of corn into the pond and in several days they came out in a large spring ten or fifteen miles away.

It was told by my grandfather and many people that during the "bad days" after the Civil War, bodies were dumped into the pond and never found. Nothing was ever seen but their black hats floating on the muddy water.

The pond was a mystery but it provided some good stories at the country store when the conversation got around to mysterious places.

When I was a small boy, I would go to the pond with my father and grandfather and just sit on the bank and look at the water and listen to these stories they had to tell. It was an exciting time and they seemed to like to talk about it.

Then we might go back to the country store at Dora,

Missouri, or a few miles on down to Birdtown, Missouri, and strike up a conversation about where we had been and hear more stories about this mystery.

Taylor's Cave

This story was told to me by my grandmother, Tennessee James Martin, who died at the age of eighty-one in 1941. She had heard it from her father.

Even though it is an old story, it comes to life often, even today. Perhaps this story came from the frontier period in Missouri and was strengthened by the Civil War activities, because it was said that it was used by Confederate troops during and after the war.

The mystery of the cave's location has been of concern to many people of Ozark County, Missouri, for many years. Talk of the cave and its location comes alive often and about everyone who is a true native takes their turn telling a version of how it was used and how it can be found.

Many people believe that the cave is located on the Northfork of White River about three miles above the junction of the Northfork and Bryant Creek.

My great-grandfather was a farmer in this community before and during the Civil War. He was a close friend to a man named Taylor. It is said that Grandfather and other people of the community noticed from time to time Mr. Taylor and other men who were strangers in the community making repeated trips to West Plains, Missouri, the nearest town, in wagons. The wagons went to town empty but came back with heavy covered loads.

At other times they went loaded and came back empty. People began to talk. Was Mr. Taylor moonshining? What was he up to? Much gossip spread over the community about what Mr. Taylor was taking into and out of the community and where was he taking it. Many people believed that he had a hide-away-cave where he was storing his loot or whatever it was in the covered wagons. Many people began to say that he was a bad man and no good for the community.

A few years later after much of the gossip had died down, Mr. Taylor came calling on Grandpa James. During his visit he mentioned that he wanted Grandpa to see a cave he had found that few people knew about. Grandpa was delighted and soon accepted the invitation. He was blindfolded before they started. On the trip they crossed several rivers, probably the same river several times; they went up and down hills. The wagon bumped over rocks and ditches and up more hills. All this took about five or six hours, according to Grandpa.

Finally, they stopped and entered a cave. Inside, the blindfold was removed and there before his eyes were hundreds of large barrels of silver coins, large slabs of silver and machines for making money. After Grandpa had viewed the inside of the cave, he was blindfolded again. The trip back to his house was about the same as the trip to the cave. He tried for years to return by the same route which he thought he could remember but he went without ever finding anything.

From that time to the present, people have looked for the cave. Some say the entrance is covered by a huge flat rock. Others say the entrance is no larger than a man's body.

Some argue that about one hundred feet north of the cave is a large rock with an arrow carved on it pointing toward the entrance. Some say that there are a series of carvings on rocks in the shape of Indian arrowheads which lead to the cave. Others say that a spring of water is near the entrance to the cave. Many believe that near the mouth of the cave is a pile of large rocks three or four feet high.

I'll have to admit that when I walk over these Ozark hills and see a hole in the side of a hill or piles of large rock or a large rock standing out of a branch bed, I wonder if that just might be the entrance to the riches of silver.

This is an interesting subject in the conversation of Ozark cracker-barrel philosophers, and will, no doubt, live on as a legend of a strange or mysterious place, unless someone finds it.

The Horse Thief

My sources for the following information were my father, E.C. Decker (1895-1990), of Tecumseh, Missouri; the *Unpublished Memoirs* of the late Charles Owens (1887-1984), of Gainesville and Ava, Missouri, and my own information that I have picked up over the years from hearing the story told and retold.

In 1898 a man moved to the Ozarks with his wife and three small children from Oklahoma, Kansas or somewhere West. He settled in a small cabin near the Dora, Missouri Ridge. His cabin was near Althea Springs and Patrick Bridge on the North Fork of White River. The story spread that he was a horse thief and was running from the law. Some local residents found out about this and made him pay them not to tell Ozark County authorities. As time went on they demanded more money. He asked them to produce a letter they said they had from a sheriff in another state. So the two men brought the letter.

"That's not within a thousand miles of where I thought," he said. "I'll kill you both for you are trying to frame me." He pulled a shotgun and shot them but neither was killed.

Soon a posse was formed and they along with the sheriff

and his deputy went to the man's house to arrest him. They did not take a warrant. The man would not come out so they surrounded the house. Some hid behind trees, some behind a chicken house and some behind rocks.

Most of the men had got whiskey before they got there and were drunk. It was about midnight when they got to his house. It was a dark night so they decided to wait until morning to arrest him because they expected him to put up a fight.

But some could not wait until morning so they began to fire into the house. The man returned the fire. Soon a deputy sheriff crept to the house, went into a room, came out, and as he passed a window the man on the inside shot him dead.

The fight continued even after the deputy was killed. One man who was sitting behind a tree lit a cigarette. This was about fifty yards away. When the light from his match flared, a bullet from the house ground into the tree and pieces of bark flew high in the air.

The next morning another deputy crawled close to the house and began to talk to the man inside. He told him if he would come out without his guns, he would promise that no one would harm him.

"They're tryin' to mob me," the man said.

But he finally threw out three guns and walked out, and got in the wagon seat with the sheriff. The sheriff gave the man a forty-five and said, "Boys, I'm taking this man to jail. If anybody tries to stop me, they are dead."

They took him to Gainesville, Missouri, the County Seat of Ozark County. Feelings ran strong for several days. But when people heard the entire story, they began to take the side of the accused.

One man tried to slip into the jail and shoot the prisoner,

but he was stopped. So the County hired a man to guard the jail day and night.

Soon the word got out that the man's wife and children were starving, so a man from Gainesville went to the cabin on North Fork River and brought them to his hotel to stay. Many people in town resented this but the hotel owner paid no attention to them.

It was decided to have the man's trial as soon as possible since tensions were so high in the county and the town of Gainesville. So in about three weeks the trial was held. A jury set the man free.

The sheriff took the man to his home to keep someone from killing him. Some had said that he would never leave Gainesville, Missouri, alive.

The next day after the trial the hotel owner and the sheriff took their hacks and took the man and his family about a day's drive north. It has been said that they put them out at the town of Mansfield, Missouri.

Uncle Charlie Owens was a young man at the time this all happened. He said, "The old jail was made out of logs. I was in town the morning they brought him in and I went to the jail to see him. He was sitting on a stool chair in the middle of the room and his coon skin cap was on another stool beside him. I felt so sorry for him I almost cried."

The man was never heard of again. However, several years later it was told that a young man thought to be his son returned to the area. Certain men in the Dora, Lawndale and Elijah, Missouri area got nervous every time this was mentioned.

Most of this story is true. However, it changes some every time it is told. Although it happened in 1898, it was retold and talked about every few years. The last time I heard it mentioned was in the late 1970s.

The man who at first was called a horse thief became a folk hero in the community and people talked about it for years. This is an example of a mysterious event that caused much excitement for many people.

The "Blue Man" or "Wild Man" of the Ozarks

My father and uncles who were born and raised around Dora and Birdtown, Missouri, told me this strange story. They heard it from their father and from conversations at the country store or anywhere people wanted to talk about it.

It seems that this strange creature of a man roamed over the hills and river valleys in Douglas, Howell and Ozark Counties in southern Missouri.

The three main rivers of this area are the North Fork of White River, Bryant Creek and Spring Creek, which is a tributary of the North Fork.

This all started shortly after the Civil War. Most people hunted and trapped along the rivers and over the hills. It was not uncommon for several people to be out in the woods and along the rivers every day.

One cold winter day about 1875 a man and his son were hunting on a ridge between North Fork of White River and Spring Creek. As they walked along the ridge, they noticed large tracks in the snow. They thought it might be a bear track since they had seen bear in that area before. But they were amazed at its size. This made them wonder if it was a bear track or the track of something much larger. As the father and the son walked on, they became more cautious and often tried to walk quietly.

Suddenly from the top of a hill they heard a roaring scream that sounded like a wild animal in pain. They hid behind a large rock near the trail and waited. As they glanced at the top of the hill, they saw a large man with no clothing except some sort of skin around his waist. His body was covered with black hair which took on a blue color as the sun hit it.

When the big man saw them coming, he ran away up the hill yelling and screaming as he went.

The man and his son went back to their community and told what they had seen. So several men from the community went to try and track the wild man and capture him or at least get a better look at him. They spread out over the ridges and along the rivers. One time they saw him in the far distance but he was too far away to get a shot at him or even a good look.

For several nights after this search people could hear wild screams during the night. They were scared and kept their guns near by and loaded. The next morning they would wake up to find small animals such as goats, small pigs and chickens killed and partly eaten.

But for several years no one saw or heard anything about the Wild Man. But they continued to talk about that man.

About five years later in about 1880 he was heard of again several miles on west along Bryant Creek. This was at least twenty-five miles from where he was sighted on the North Fork earlier. People began to lose small animals and chickens. Often they would hear a wild, death-like scream from the darkness of the night. During the day they searched and searched but found nothing.

It was about this time that some timber workers moved into the area from southwest Missouri and northern Arkansas. They came to cut stave bolts and walnut logs. Since they got most of what they ate from the woods, they brought their hunting dogs with them. One day they were working on stave bolts and heard their dogs barking over on the next ridge. They thought they sounded like they were bayed but when they got to the dogs, they were treed. These timber men told the people around Dora, Missouri, that they had treed a man who looked wild and scared. Like before, he was almost naked. The men said that they tried to talk to him but he just screamed and yelled at them. The timber men called off their dogs and went back to work. They did not bother the man because he had not bothered them.

From about 1880 to 1905 the Wild Man came back at different times and was heard of in Ozark, Douglas and Howell Counties in Missouri. Everybody talked about him. Most of them were anxious to know more about him. They carried guns when they were in the woods. They examined places in caves that looked like someone had slept there.

In the 1920s people in this area became excited about the Wild Man again. They kept their small animals in pens close to the house and never left the house without a gun. Some even thought the Wild Man was spying on them. One night at church a woman screamed out right in the middle of church that the man was at one of the windows. Some said it was the glimpse of a shadow of an angel since it cast a blue light. Others said it was the devil lookin' in.

One winter in the 1920s several men butchered twelve hogs one day. The next morning large chunks of meat were torn from hams and large tracks were seen near the smokehouse door.

And one young man who was out late one night swore that the Wild Man screamed at him from the community cemetery as he passed it.

One elderly man told my grandfather that he heard that before the Revolutionary War that a French fur trader came through the area with a beautiful Spanish woman and traded her to an Indian chief for some furs and food. She lived in the woods for years. From this came a people half Indian and half Spanish. When settlers moved in around 1820-1850, these strange people disappeared. Many thought they traveled south to the Boston Mountains in Arkansas. This elderly man said that a few people like the Wild Man and some of his descendants had been left behind.

Chapter 3

Ozark Individuals

One could find an interesting individual in about any local community. No individual was perfect and they all knew it. Some were laughed at; some were thought to be no-good citizens. Some gossiped about what others did at church, or what they didn't do. Many were praised. They made heroes out of some. But whatever they did or thought, they didn't want any outsider coming in and criticizing anyone. They were proud of their own, no matter what they did.

New-comers or foreigners, as some were called, were treated kindly and respected as long as they didn't interfere with the customs. Hill folks didn't like quick change. As long as these new people kept their distance, didn't ask too many questions, and minded their own business, they were accepted.

Individuals played a great part in the amusement of the people as they talked on the streets of small towns, as they met at the country store on Saturday or as they visited in other's homes after church on Sunday.

Young children, peddlers, drummers, tramps, outlaws, preachers, bachelors, "widder" women, church leaders and granny women received most of the discussion.

Depression Time in the Ozarks

(This includes the story of a lady who as a little girl during the Depression was determined to survive and to help herself but most of all to help her family.)

During the Great Depression most people in the Ozarks were very poor, but they didn't know it. Most of their neighbors were in the same fix. However they were proud despite their poverty.

One man in northern Arkansas told me that his mama hung meat skins on the front porch so they would hit the kids in the face as they left for school. This way the teacher would see the grease on their faces and think that they had had breakfast. I think he was joking but they were proud.

Another man in southern Missouri also made a joke about his family's condition. He said that they were so poor that his sister got hurt one morning at breakfast. She fell out of a "simmon" tree.

During the Depression in the Ozarks the federal government had a mattress making project. The government furnished all the materials for making the mattress. All the people had to do was to go to a selected location, usually a country schoolhouse or church and make their own mattress for no charge. But many people would not participate. They said they did not want anything from the government for nothing. One man said he would not sleep on anything FDR had anything to do with.

Maxine Field, a wonderful lady who lives in Mountain View, Arkansas, tells of growing up during the Depression near Big Flat, Arkansas. Now Maxine and her husband Lew live in a beautiful home in Mountain View.

She remembers the conditions in that part of the Ozarks. They were hard workers, proud, had fun but had to struggle to survive.

As a young girl she cared for her younger brothers and sister and helped her parents make a living. While her father was living, he worked for fifty cents a day. Quite sometime after he died, her mother got $9 a month from his veteran's pension.

She hewed crossties with a broad axe. She always remembered her father telling her to watch that sharp broad axe, to spread her legs so it would not cut her leg or foot.

At age fourteen she carried 100-pound sacks of shorts[3] from the road above their home. This was about a quarter mile. But she knew how to carry a heavy sack. After getting the sack onto a rock, she would bend over, get under the sack, get it by the ears and as her little brother pushed the sack, she would rise up with it on her back. They needed the shorts to feed the cow.

"I could make the chips fly with that broad axe. After we worked in the woods all day, from sunup to sundown, we were hungry. We didn't have much to eat. We made a big garden, canned food and made gravy. We liked that gravy. We made it with water because we didn't have any milk when the cow was dry. When we got to cravin' sweets, we went to the woods and ate black haws, 'possum grapes and persimmons.

"I don't know how we survived in the 30s. No one had anything except that old man on the hill. We even had trouble making a garden because we didn't have money to buy seeds to plant."

"When Daddy was alive he cut cedar posts. Got three maybe five cents for each post. Daddy's hands were so black from the cedar rosin but we helped him. His hands were so black. We helped him cut ties. This was when he was afraid I would cut myself with the sharp broad axe."

"But we could go into Big Flat and buy all the groceries we wanted for $3 or $4. But it took a lot of time and hard work to make that much money."

"Daddy, my brother and me, we worked for a man doing hard work. I mean hard work. It was about three and a half miles to his place. We got up before daylight, took a torch to see. Had to use the torch because we didn't have kerosene light. The man put us to work in "new ground". Couldn't plow it. It was too rocky. We just pulled the weeds with our hands. We worked till sundown. By the time we got home, it was dark again. We got $12 a month for this."

"I want you to know, my brother, my daddy and I, all of us, $12 a month. Well there wasn't anything better, nothing. I tell you people didn't have anything. If there had been any work, thirty or forty miles away, we couldn't have got there. No cars, no horses, no mules to ride. We were stuck there."

"Catching 'coons, 'possums and other wild animals was another way we got a little money. We caught them for their skins. After we killed a 'coon, we skinned him. You had to know just how to do it so as not to cut up the hide the wrong way. Daddy showed us how. We stretched the skin on a board which was smaller and smooth at one end for the front of the hide. After we got the skin on just as tight as we could, we nailed it at the ends so as not to damage the skin. But we didn't have any nails. So we would go to old houses or houses that had burned and collect all the nails we could. They were burned and brittle but they held the hide on the board pretty well. Also we whittled small arrows of cedar to lace the hide on a framework of arrows. The tiny arrows were delicate so we had to be careful in order to get them in so the hide would be tight. The hide had to be tight."

"We got most of our wild animals by trapping them. We had some double spring traps. One good way was to put a dead bird upon a limb above where we had set the trap in leaves. The bobcat or some other animal would jump to get the bird and come down on the trap and we had him."

"One time on Almas Knob near Big Flat we caught a large bobcat in a 2-spring trap. The cat had cut briars and pulled limbs to hide from us. But, boy, when we got there, he came out from there and got pretty close to me. Lunged at us. Frightened, my brother, sister and I ran and then climbed a tree. The bobcat finally broke the chain the trap was tied to. Later after getting our dog, we tracked it up to a cave but the dog wouldn't go into the cave after it. And we never found it."

"Now let me tell you something about school. School was just three months a year. Children were needed to help with crops and cotton picking and so forth. School was three miles away up on the mountain. We lived down in a canyon. The school house was actually on the side of the mountain with woods all around. Often, we went out in the woods to get firewood for the school."

"We walked about a quarter of a mile to get water. Didn't have any out-houses. Girls went to the front in the woods and boys went to the back. This was understood. When we raised our hands to go to the bathroom, we had to know which way to go."

"When it got hot in the fall, we moved out of the old school house and down the hillside and built a brush arbor. It was cooler. We dragged them old benches down the hill and set them up. Carried that old blackboard down and nailed it to a couple of trees. Sometimes we would drag them old benches out in the creek and sit in them with our feet in the water."

"Had some teachers who were good. One thing for sure they did not spare the rod. You'd get the tar whipped out of you if you didn't do what they said. They'd take you up in front of the class and you'd get the fire whipped out of you. You were darn glad to get back to your seat."

"I did something one time. I don't remember what it was and the teacher hit me with a switch on my back. My dress had a low neck; my aunt had given it to me, and that switch wrapped around my neck and made a deep red circle where it had gone around my neck."

"There was a girl who sat beside me and she was all the time drawing some old crazy animal with all kinds of heads on them you could ever see. She'd stick that picture right up under my nose and keep on till I got tickled. I'd try not to laugh. I'd almost choke myself. I didn't want to get in trouble so I would put my hand up right quick to go to the bathroom."

"The teacher would say: 'What? Are you wanting permission for Maxine, to laugh?' Then I'd just start laughing like everything and he'd cut me with that switch. And dad burn her, she'd just shut up and not laugh like she hadn't done anything. And there I was just laughin' and laughin'. He never got on to her."

"So one day I asked him to move me away from her. He asked what she was doing. But I couldn't ever tell him and get her into trouble. I just said she giggles a lot. Finally, he did make her move away from me."

"I'm sure this teacher was all right. But in some ways he was a little strange, maybe a mental block. His actions were a little bit on the crazy side."

"One day my mom said, 'Maxine when you come home from school tonight, you bring some pine knots so we can start a fire.' She said, 'Don't come home without any.'"

"Well, it was snowing--big snow. The teacher told us to get out in the woods and along the road and gather all the pine knots we could find. That snow was deep and we didn't have any overshoes, just gunnysacks wired around our feet. But my cousin and all the rest of us kids got out and got all the pine knots we could find and we piled them in the corner of the school house in a big box."

"At the end of the day I asked the teacher for a couple of them pine knots. I told him my mama would whip me when I got home if I didn't have any and we had piled up a bunch in the corner of the school house."

I said, "If I can just have a couple."

"No! No! No! No!" he said.

So I cut it down to one. "Just let me have one to get the fire started," I said.

"No! No! No! No! We need them right here."

"I knew if I went home without one, I would get a whippin'. I told my friend Darlene that I had to have a pine knot. I didn't want to go home. But I didn't have any place else to go. But I knew I had to go home. I told Darlene that if we could just get inside the school house, we could get us one."

"Darlene said we should go down the hillside and hide and when he left, we could pry open a window, get inside and get one."

"So we went down the hill and got under a big cedar tree and waited for him to leave. It was cold in the snow and we almost froze to death."

"Finally he came out of the school house and bolted the door with a big lock and took off."

"We waited awhile till we thought that he was gone quite a way and then went up to the school house."

"We looked in a window and saw that he had poured water all around the stove so nothing would get on fire."

I said, "Darlene there is no way we can get in there. There is no way we can get any window open."

"I finally remembered that where a table stood that underneath were some loose boards. If we could just get underneath, maybe we could push those boards up and crawl through the crack and come up right smack under the table. When we were in we could get us some pine knots and get out the same way. So we did that and got in and got us two pine knots."

"But in the meantime the teacher came back for something before we could get out. We could see him looking through a window."

"I got you! I got you! I got you!" he said.

"But by the time he got in the door, me and Darlene had gone through that crack in the floor, under the house, and gone the same way we got in."

"I took two pine knots home and told Mama what I had done."

She said, "If he w'ars you out, I ain't going to say anything."

"The next day he brought us up before the whole school. "That's just the way it was."

"As I have stated before we were very poor. If people up on the hill had known about us, they would have done something, if they could. But they didn't know. We didn't complain. We just worked and tried to get anything to survive."

"I remember that up on the hill was a Triple-C Camp.[4] They would throw away stuff that was no good to them. So we could search through what they had thrown away and find bread that had molded. We would scrape off the mold and eat it."

There was one thing that seemed to stand in Maxine's memory more than any other. I could tell that this bothered her more than the whippings, the hunger or the hard work. I could tell that this was something that she would never forget.

"One girl in school whose father had a store had bubble gum. She brought it to school and chewed it and blew bubbles every day. I watched her and watched her. I wanted some of that gum so bad I could taste it. She'd just chew it and blow it and flaunt it all around."

"So I thought maybe I can make me some. So I got some pine rosin and some sweet gum sap which was waxy and had a sweet taste. And I got me some green briar berries. The membrane on the green briar berry's seeds was waxy and made the gum stick together. It took many berries to get enough of this membrane but I found them. So I had bubble gum all my own. I took it to school and chewed and chewed and got to where I could blow a pretty good bubble. That helped me a lot. Now she was not the only one that could chew gum and blow bubbles. I had me a good time with that gum and it made me feel good."

One of the major problems that faced Maxine and her family was the death of her father during all these hard times. He was a good man and worked so hard to provide what he could for his family. But he contracted malaria from wading and diving in the Buffalo River looking for mussel shells to take to market. He became so sick but there was no money for medicine. In a short time he died. This placed more responsibility on the little girl and ended any income for the family for about six months until the Mother got the veteran's widow pension of $9 a month.

But Maxine went on working and helping her family.

She kept on doing what she had to do. She loved her family and knew that they had to have her help.

All these experiences she had as a child during this period of our history showed her determination, her ingenuity and her willingness to work hard for those she loved.

This reflects how a people battled the hard times of the Depression and took care of their own. Even to this day she has little respect for the person who complains about their lot in life and does little to help themselves.

Peddlers

During the time of the Civil War into the 1940s peddlers roamed through the country selling their products. Most peddlers would make about any kind of deal. They would trade cherry flavored cold drink mixes for old batteries, hens, roosters, rabbits, a mess of fish, scrap iron or a bushel of sweet potatoes. Maybe they wouldn't cheat one on purpose but they usually came out well when they made the trade.

But what could a Father or Mother do when the peddler waved around those bottles of colored mixes that he said tasted so good on a hot summer day? What could they do when the peddler said that this little bottle would color the icing for fifty cakes the most beautiful pink in the world? They did what they had to do. They either came up with the money to buy it or they looked around the house for something to trade. They were proud to do some little something for their family. And the peddler knew their weakness.

The peddler's method of travel was by hack, by covered wagon or in later years a beaten up old car or truck. But whatever it was, it was the type of transportation that pointed them out in any area so that anyone could look out the window and tell at a glance if the peddler was coming.

He was a man who was always welcome. He usually stayed for at least one meal which he ate as if he had not eaten in a week. And hotel reservations did not bother him at all for he always managed to make it to a good bed at a customer's house just before dark.

Small children got a great excitement from the peddler's visit. His long, heavy open wire carriage and dark black case were filled with fragrant odors of spices and perfumes. The gaily colored boxes of even the "barbed wire" ointment were sights to behold. And as he chanted his advertisement over colored boxes of coconut pie mix, nature remedy, perfumed soap, salve for cow's udders or fine grain black pepper, small children huddled around with amazement. For the peddler was a treat, an event, something to look forward to not only for the children but the adults.

One peddler who came to our house was a preacher. He did a good business, especially with the members of his church. He was welcome to spend the night with about anyone for there would always be a good discussion of the Bible after supper.

Another man who made his living by selling such products stands out in the memory of many Ozark people. Old Andy always based his sales talks on the basis of his wife's or his sister-in-law's use of the product.

"Nancy. No it was sis. No it was Nancy. Er maybe it was both of them used this female tonic and they haven't had a pain of any kind for six months," he would say.

One elderly man in one Ozark community must have been convinced that the woman's tonic was good. One day at the local store he asked if they had any of that tonic described for women that the peddler sold. "I've taken six bottles of that Miss Janie's Remedy and I haven't felt better in my life. Hit completely cured the rheumatism in my left knee. But that damn peddler ain't been by for two weeks now and I am out."

In addition to the peddlers who made house calls, there was the medicine man who made gatherings such as public auctions or picnics. His product was some type of medicine, a cure-all, which sold well.

There were peddlers who sold newspaper subscriptions. Sometimes if the farmer wanted to pay cash, a reward of some valuable article such as an ironing board will be given free of charge. Most papers and magazines such as *Grit, Illustrated Companion, Kansas City Star* and *Comfort* offered valuable world news, stories, market reports and interesting editorials which farmers enjoyed.

Drummers

Drummers were like peddlers in many ways, except they sold their products to rural stores. They sold coats, shoes, overshoes, dresses, overalls, just about anything called "dry goods."

Those who visited stores in rural southwest Missouri and northern and northwest Arkansas were usually from Springfield, Missouri. So when they traveled seventy or eighty miles during the week, they were ready for a good meal about anytime and a good bed at night. So most drummers spent the night with the owner of the store he had visited late in the day or with some family he happened to know in the community.

Drummers were good company. People liked to hear them talk about life in the big city and what was going on in other areas of the Ozarks.

Tramps

From the Civil War through the 1930's, tramps were frequent visitors to country homes and villages. They were people without a home. All the tramps I ever saw were men. They were mysterious to everyone, especially small children. They were strange to dogs, also. Any dog that had any breeding at all could sense a tramp a mile away and gave them the scare of their lives. Any dog seemed to just not like tramps.

One tramp who was called Old Jim made his rounds through southern Missouri and northern Arkansas for many years. His only possessions were a few pots and pans which were slung over his shoulder in a gunny sack. He slept in barns, caves and the woods. His only means of livelihood was getting a free meal from the kitchen door of a rural farm home or if it was absolutely necessary cutting wood for a man who insisted that he work just a little before he would give him food.

Most everyone thought of tramps as harmless people. They didn't bother anyone except when they were hungry. As Old Jim walked along a country road or slowly cut some farmer's wood, he must have had a dream of something better on down the road for he would constantly sing a song that went something like this: "Live in a big house, board in the kitchen; live in a big house, board in the kitchen."

Outlaws

For many years in the Ozarks people would tell you one of two things about the most notorious outlaw in this area, Jesse James. They would say they were related to him, especially if their name was James, or that he was still living somewhere in the state of Arkansas.

But Jesse and Frank James were in the Ozarks, no doubt. Many people can tell of several hideouts that the James boys used as they came in and went out of Missouri and Arkansas from Oklahoma.

One story tells about Jesse and his gang coming through the Ozarks from Kansas after they had robbed a bank in that state. The law got close to them and they were forced to throw many sacks of silver coins in a ditch. The money was never found. However, many people believe it is somewhere among the rocks of the hills yet.

Some people say that a few outlaws worked out of the state of Arkansas. They would raid across the line at night and escape back into the hills before the next day. However, much of this type of robbery was the work of people in the area because it was a tendency to say all bad things in Missouri were done by someone in the state to the south.

Preachers

Ozark people take their religion seriously but they have had their fun with preachers. Many of the stories were, perhaps, true, but some may have been "stretched" just a little by some of the less religious brothers and sisters.

One story is told about a preacher Jim who was fond of chicken legs. One Sunday this preacher had gone home with a family for Sunday dinner. Now this family had just finished digging a new well and, naturally, the preacher wanted to take a look at it. So just before dinner he went to the well, bent over to get a good view and dropped both upper and lower plates of his false teeth into the deep well. Everyone became startled. What on earth would he do? What could they do? Pandemonium broke out among the family. Poor preacher! He could not even continue the meeting without his teeth and worse than that he could not eat.

Several methods of getting the teeth were discussed. Other neighbors were called in. Soon the entire congregation was at the well. Sisters prayed that the good Lord would show the way. Brothers bent over the well in desperate deliberation.

Finally, one wise man of the group, as a joke perhaps, suggested that they tie a leg of a chicken, which had been cooked for dinner, to a string and lower it into the clear water in the well and catch the teeth. So it was tried in desperation. At the very moment that the chicken leg hit the water, the teeth grabbed it and held on for dear life. The wise brother gently pulled the string and brought the teeth to the top.

Thus the teeth were recovered and it was said that despite the excitement the preacher ate the darndest dinner and preached the best sermon that night that anyone in those parts could remember.

This story was enjoyed over the area around Tecumseh, Missouri, for years and became known as the story, "The Preacher and the Drumstick."

Another story about preachers was known as "The Day Grandma Brought the Preacher Home from Church." It was a custom in the '30s and '40s to feed the preacher now and then. It was impossible at that time to take the preacher out to a café to eat. There was no place to go. So we had him at our house.

Grandma lived with us after Grandpa died until her death twelve years later. She was a deeply religious person. She had read the entire Bible, maybe more than once. She went to church every Sunday and now and then she felt that we should feed the preacher.

It was on a Wednesday that she made her intentions clear. She instructed my mother that several things had to be done to get ready for the preacher's visit on Sunday. So at her directions we scrubbed all the floors in the rather large house. They washed the curtains and the windows. They washed the porches. They re-washed the dishes and shined them. They shined the pots and pans. They shook the rugs. After about two days everything looked good and clean, even though it was clean to begin with.

Friday was the day to talk about Sunday dinner. Usually, Grandma insisted we have brown beans, cornbread, fried chicken, turnips, fried apples, fried potatoes, side pork, peas, corn-on-the-cob, biscuits, chicken gravy, sausage and cherry pie.

"Whatever we have, we must have fried chicken and cherry pie. All preachers like that," she would say.

On this Sunday morning we got up early because there were still many things to do.

"Take this chicken leg hook and go out to the chicken yard and get one of the best roosters you can find. We'll cook him for dinner. Hurry, now. We've got to get him ready so we can start frying him just as soon as we get home from church," my mother told me.

Well, the leg hook was easy. I could catch a rooster in just a few minutes. All I had to do was slip the long stiff wire that had a hook bent in one end, up through the twenty or thirty young white Leghorn roosters and pull it just a little and it would slip around the leg of one. Then all I had to do was ring his neck and take him to the house.

But I had a different idea that day. I had used the leg hook many times before and that wasn't too exciting for a nine-year-old boy. So I got me a handful of rocks, singled out what I thought was a nice rooster, shooed him away from the rest and swung with the rocks at his head.

Well, I got my rooster with the second or third throw, wrung his neck or chopped it off with the axe, I don't remember which, and took him to Grandma and Mama who would do the rest.

This rooster fried well. So with all the other food, we had a feast the preacher seemed to enjoy. In fact, he ate again before we headed out for Sunday night services.

And, it seemed that Grandma felt she had done something good for the Lord for she had given the preacher two good meals. She seemed happier all week as I can remember.

We had some preachers who would preach three or four hours. Everyone would get tired, especially the children. Children would get hungry, need to go the bathroom but we couldn't. We had to sit there. We could not go to sleep or distract the church in any way.

We got to know the long-winded preachers and would ask on Sunday morning who was going to preach that day. Sometimes we didn't have a full-time preacher. A different one would come in every Sunday. So if the one who preached a long time was going to be there, I often got sick just before church and Mom would stay home with me. I liked the singing and everything but that three or four hours of preaching got tiresome.

One preacher came into our community in southern Missouri one time and on the first night asked if everyone believed in the hereafter. Everyone raised their hands.

The preacher said, "Well, I do too. I'm here after your money." So he set up a $1 row, a $5 row and a $10 row.

Another preacher came back year after year to the Nottinghill, Missouri area and stayed with the same family each time. Now the family with whom he stayed was noted for their cleanliness and the Mother of the family washed his white shirt every day. He just had one shirt and it was worn so much that it would hardly hold together without the thick starch she put on it. She ironed it with an old iron heated on the stove and still didn't scorch the shirt.

Candidates for Office

Candidates for county office had to do about anything to get a vote. Some time during local picnics, candidates were given an chance to express their views and solicit the vote of those present. The most popular candidates were those who promised everybody something and after their speech announced that if everyone would go to the lunch stand there would be hamburgers for all voters and their children. No weak creature could stand the rush to the free meal. They pushed, shoved, laughed and ate ten times more than they wanted, just because it was free, free on that candidate.

Sometime in the 1940s on Election Day in August in Richland Township in Ozark County, Missouri several candidates were at the polling place. It seems that the county always designated Birdtown, Missouri as the voting place. Two men who were running for an office seemed to be in a tight race over the county so it was important for them to try and get the most votes in this township which had a rather large number of voters.

People came early and visited but they did not get in a hurry to vote. They could spend all the time they wanted just visiting and maybe getting some treats from the candidates.

About two o'clock one candidate decided to make his move. He got up on a tree stump and announced in a loud voice that the load of watermelons that everyone could see was on him. So he got in the wagon and began to cut the large melons in quarters. He made a point to say that everyone could come back as many times as they wished but one quarter of these were about all anyone could eat.

After the voters had eaten all the melons they wanted, the other candidate decided he must do something so he announced that people could go into the store and get all the canned goods they wanted, on him. He bought all the canned goods in the store. So they went in and carried out armloads of cans like carrying sticks of wood. Soon all the canned goods were gone.

But the melons and the cans of food must have been equally popular because when they counted the votes that night the two men had about the same number of votes.

A candidate never came to a picnic or any type of gathering in fine clothing. That wouldn't work at all. "Look at that feller all 'tiggered' up. I don't like the looks of them fine clothes. May think he's better than the rest of us. I'll not vote for him. I'll just cast my vote for Ole Rimey Peters. He's more like ordinary folks," many would say.

A candidate had to watch his actions at a picnic, for example, or any other place. He'd sure better bring some money, his pipe, a few cigarette papers and a twist of chewin' tobacco, because there was sure to be some voter who would want a few crumbs. When a candidate 'lectioneered with a man who was a chewer, he better chew too. When he was with a roll-your-own-man, he better roll his own. When he met a man who liked a little drink, it was always better if he had a little drink too. But he had to be careful about drinking for there were a few voters in the Ozarks who didn't look favorably on a drinkin' candidate.

After the polls closed at the township voting place, the candidates and many other interested citizens made their way to the county seat where the votes from each township were counted.

The candidate for an office who won lost his hat. It was a custom to get the winner's hat along with other winner's hats and burn them in the courthouse lawn or in the street of the county seat. Some candidates didn't wear their hats or at least they didn't wear their best hat. However I have seen some good Stetson hats go up in smoke that were taken from a winner who just wanted to be a good sport and let the boys have some fun.

Candidates for school board positions wanted to win but this office didn't pay a salary. These elections were held at the local schoolhouse and anyone who was an eligible voter could run or vote. Voters would just write their choice on a tiny piece of paper they were given and place it in a hat that was passed around by someone who was usually a volunteer. Several times candidates were accused of placing pieces of paper under the hat band of the hat that was passed to the voters with their name on it. Or they had some of their supporters to do this for them. They had to make sure that the right hat was passed and the man who passed the hat was on their side so he would shake the hat well, pull down the band well so all the votes would fall out. At one school election in the southern Missouri Ozarks two candidates got more votes than there were voters present. People knew all this was going on but they didn't say much about it.

Although school board members got no pay, no salary, they were accused of taking a little money or something from a person who wanted to teach the school for the next year. There were three directors or board members so a teacher could get the job with two votes. It was told that in one school district in the southern Missouri Ozarks that some teaching jobs went as high as $50 which was a lot of money in the '30s. One board member was said to have gotten three sheep and ten shocks of fodder for his vote.

Granny-Women

Granny-women were respected in the Ozarks. Many people thought that they were better to have around during childbirth than most doctors.

When they were needed, someone went after them and they came. If a doctor was there, they helped deliver the baby. They wiped the after-birth off the baby, washed it, saw that it nursed and wrapped it in a soft blanket. If the doctor was not there, they did everything themselves.

The granny-woman who helped deliver babies in the community where I grew up was a heavy fat woman. She was just right to provide a soft bed on her lap for a newborn baby.

She stayed around as long as she was needed and could be called back at any time. She was not on a tight schedule.

She did not charge for her services. This seemed to be her way of saying I have the ability to do this and I want to help.

Ozark Mountain Doctors and Dentists

From the time of the earliest white settlement well into the 1950s, the Ozarks was blessed with country doctors. Some of them got their degree in medicine by correspondence course schools; some just seemed to become a doctor and some studied and graduated from excellent medical schools. Most of the doctors were blessed with granny-women or mid-wives that were found in about every community. They helped the doctors deliver babies, "set up" with the sick and just acted as the doctor's nurse. In fact, I have been told that some Ozark Mountain men would not let a doctor deliver a baby at their house but called for a granny woman. They did not want a man messin' around with their wives' female "parts" even if she was having a baby.

The doctors usually set up an office in a small village so people could come when they were able to travel or when the doctor was too busy to come to their house. But the doctor also traveled over the country to people's houses when they were sick. They traveled by buggy, hack or rode a horse.

My wife's grandfather, Dr. John H. Small was a doctor from the early 1900s well into the 1940s at Lutie, Missouri, which is in south central Missouri not far from the Arkansas border. One time a man called him and said his wife was very sick and would he come and doctor her. Now this man lived with his family in a very remote area of the hills so the doctor went by horseback. He carried his medical bag and a change of clothing in his saddle bags.

When he got to the man's house, it was dark. The only light was a coal oil lamp, which probably had a sooty globe. The man led him into a small, dark bedroom where his wife lay in bed. The doctor could not see her very well so he got down close to her face as the man held the dim light. When he got close to her face, he saw that she had smallpox, which was very contagious.

Now Dr. Small had an invalid wife and two small children at home and he was afraid he would carry the dreaded disease back to them. So he took all the precautions he could think of.

After he gave the woman some medicine, he asked the man to put on a kettle of water and get it boiling hot. He pulled off his clothing and with lye soap and the water as hot as he could stand it, he washed his entire body. Then he put on the fresh change of clothing he had in his saddlebags and burned his other clothing.

Neither he nor his family at home took the smallpox.

In the 1940s I had an experience with a "bad" cold. My mother and grandmother made me wear a poultice of fried onions, gave me horehound cough medicine, painted my throat with iodine and had a neighbor who smoked a strong pipe to blow smoke in my mouth and ears, but nothing helped. So my dad took me to the nearest doctor about twenty miles away. But unfortunately the doctor was not there but his son who was about twenty-five years old was keeping shop. I remember my dad telling the doctor's son why we were there. So the son looked serious for a few minutes and then began filling a sack or poke they usually used for sacking candy with some type of medicine.

He gave no directions and said nothing. So my dad just paid him and we started home. As soon as I could I looked at the medicine for I was not feeling any better. The pills were flat with a mark running across the middle. They didn't look like any cold pills I had ever seen but I took one out of the candy poke and began to chew on it. It looked like a cough drop I had seen once before so I let several melt in my mouth before we got home.

That night I remember I didn't feel very well. But I went to school the next day and took my medicine with me. Now and then I would take one and let it melt in my mouth. They didn't taste that good but I wanted to get rid of that cold.

My teacher saw what I was doing and about an hour after noon he told me that maybe I shouldn't take so many. He said that they looked something like the new drug, sulfa, that doctors were giving to some people.

That night I took a high fever, got sick at my stomach and talked crazy, they said. I knew I felt real sick. I was worse not better.

The next day dad took me back to the doctor but he was still gone but his son who had doctored me with the pills was still there. Dad told him about how I had had a bad night and that I had eaten about all of the pills in the candy poke.

"Oh, yeah! Don't' take too many of them pills. That is that new sulfa drug. Might make you sick if you take too much," he said.

Country doctors were not afraid to try anything to save a person's life even if they often did not have adequate equipment to work with. The story is told of a man who lived near Tecumseh, Missouri who had cut his leg with an ax. He waited several days before he went to the doctor. He soaked the cut in kerosene or coal oil each day but it seemed to hurt worse each day. When he finally did go to the doctor, the cut had become infected. After the doctor examined the cut and the infection, he decided that the infection had spread so far that the leg would have to be removed.

So he gave the man ether and took what looked like a hand saw and sawed the man's leg off well above the infected area. The doctor kept the man's leg in a large glass jar filled with a preservative so anyone could see what he had done. The man lived and was given a wooden leg by the doctor.

Doctors were "looked up to" in the Ozarks because they could save a life, make one have less pain and they didn't charge much. They were always welcome to stay all night and have a meal or two with the family.

Dr. Robert Sneed Small was a doctor in the Civil War and also practiced medicine at Gainesville, Missouri.

My wife's great grandfather was a doctor in the Civil War and practiced medicine in the Gainesville, Missouri, area. He, like other doctors, was proud of his horses that took him over the hills on calls. The picture above is of Dr. Small, driving a beautiful team of horses, one white, one black.

One country doctor told me about the many times he traveled to people's houses and would have to stay all night because the person was so sick he was afraid to leave them or it was night time and too dark to travel over the hills and trails to get back to his office in town.

Often it was difficult for a doctor to get paid for his services. A doctor in southern Missouri told me that when he would get ready to leave after doctoring someone, the man would say, "I don't have any money right now. I'll pay you when I can." Some would pay as soon as they could. Some would never pay and some would pay, maybe, five or ten years later. Sometimes doctors had to take anything for pay. Some took chickens, hams, potatoes or any kind of food the people had.

One doctor said he got a letter with a ten-dollar bill and a note in it. The note read, "I have owed you this for twenty years. Could have paid it sooner. Just didn't feel right about not paying you. You saved my wife's life."

One man told me about going to the dentist in the early 1900s. He had had a toothache for days. He was only about sixteen years old then but he remembered it well. He had tried everything. He had tried holding warm salt water in his mouth. He had bit hard on a rag. He had tried chewing strings. He had chewed some tobacco. He had placed a cold cloth on his jaw. Then he tried placing a hot cloth on it but nothing seemed to work. So he and his folks decided he should go to the dentist.

When he got to the dentist's office he went right in. No one was waiting. Not many people went to the dentist then. They would rather have the pain from the toothache than the pain from having it pulled.

"Yeah, that tooth is in a bad shape. I'll have to pull it. Think it is ulcerated. Looks like red streaks running up to the jaw bone. Bad shape. Shouda come before now. Wouldn't have hurt so much. Gonna be a job to get it out because of its location. Hard to get my instruments back there. Can't get a hold of it just right."

Well all of this talk didn't help much but the tooth was still hurting.

So the dentist moved him over into a cane bottom chair and went to a little box to get his instruments. The "tooth puller" looked like a pair of wire pliers with long handles. There was a little rust on the end that went into you mouth. The dentist had probably washed it off from the last time and it didn't dry.

"Sit down in this chair and open your mouth. Get a good grip on the bottom of the chair and when I start pulling the tooth, you pull up on the chair as hard as you can."

The dentist didn't give any painkiller and the tooth had long roots since it was a jaw tooth. He said the pain was terrible. He said he thought he was going to faint as the dentist twisted and pulled and twisted and pulled. But finally it came out.

"Set awhile boy. Then I think you can go. Bad tooth. Had long roots. Hard to pull. Want it?"

The dentist was just a man who had read a little about pulling teeth and maybe talked a little to a real dentist. He was not a dentist. He had no painkiller and wouldn't have known how to use it if he had had some. Someone had given him the tool to pull teeth. He was strong and when he got a good grip on a tooth and twisted it a little for awhile, it had to come out or burst into pieces.

"How much do I owe you?" the man said.

"Oh, fifty cents, I guess. That may be a little high but that was a bad tooth."

Chapter 4

Childlore

To travel into the world of children is a thrilling experience for this type of lore takes one back to one's childhood days. Like all folklore, childlore lived on the tongues of the children as they played their games, made their wishes, sang their songs and played their tricks.

Many of these amusements had been passed down to the small children from their parents and grandparents, but many were invented by the children themselves. When they needed a new game or wanted to change the rules of a game, they did not hesitate to do so. When they wanted a new song or a new verse to write in someone's autograph book, they made the words and the tune as they hopped and skipped to school.

The most popular lore of children of the Ozarks was the autograph verse and games which they played at home and at the country school.

Autograph Verses

An interesting example of childlore was the autograph verse which was popular with children from ages five to twenty. Also many adults enjoyed the funny rhymes.

The autograph book was a prized possession of many boys and girls. They were kept as a secret book and many were never opened to anyone except the owner and a close friend. They were kept in secret places and were very personal to the owner.

No doubt there has been many a thrill in a young girl's heart when she read the love words in her book which were written by a lovesick boy. Perhaps the statement, "I love you as big as the ocean," or "I love you like cows love clover," later took many an Ozark boy and girl to the preacher's house for a marriage ceremony. Or, perhaps, after they grew older, they had many delightful laughs about those "good old days" when the verse was written.

Autograph album verses in the nineteenth century were popular with all age groups. It was only in the twentieth century that it became mainly children's lore. It began about 1500 in Europe where university students liked to get their professors to inscribe some inscription in their autograph albums. It became popular in America about 1800 and it continues to the present.

These verses grew in popularity during the days of the one-room country school from about 1900 to 1950. Every student had a book or album in their desk and thought of it as one of the most important items of their school work.

The following autograph verses came from books of children with whom I attended a rural one-room school for eight years and from my students' books when I taught in a rural school for four years in southern Missouri not far from the Arkansas border.

Most autograph verses were simple, easy to understand, and had a simple rhyme which appealed to children. Many were exaggerations and many were filled with similes and metaphors.

They were examples of creativity because some were created as the children wrote and some were handed down from one generation to another.

There were many styles or subjects of autograph album verses: a "play with words", a wish, love marriage, courtship, yours till, advice, wondering what to write, remember me, writer's situation, friendship, hope, prophecy, and humor. The following that I have included are only a few of those that I have collected.

A "Play with Words"

```
        L
My  O   B   4   U
        V
        E
```

Remember A
Remember B
But C that U
Remember ME

I went to the circus tomorrow
I took a front seat in the back.
I fell from the floor to the ceiling
And broke a breast bone in my back.

I'm yours till we meet at the
```
        R
      ROAD
        A
        D
```

I'm just R/E/A/D/I/N/G
Between the lines.
And I believe that I
Love you and you love me.

2 Soon 2 Be 4 Gotten

        Dliver
        Dletter
        Dfaster
        Dbetter

Upon this hill
In a lonely spot
I write four little words
FOR-GET-ME-NOT

        FOR
  <u>GET   ME</u>
        NOT

    2 YOUNG
    <u>2 GO   </u>
    4 BOYS

Some write up and some write down
But I'll be different and write around.

    You're 2 nice
    2 B
    My friend
    4 ever.

Read	And	That	And
Up	You	I	You
And	Will	Love	Love
Down	See	You	Me

I like to be funny
Like an old, old clown.
So I'll sign my name
UPSIDE DOWN.

A Wish

I wish you health.
I wish you wealth in store.
I wish you Heaven after death.
How could I wish you more?

I wish you wealth
I wish you joy
First I wish you a baby boy
And when his hair begins to curl,
I wish you then a baby girl.
And when her hair you put in pins,
I wish you then a pair of twins.

Love

Love is like a silken cord
That binds true friends together.
And if that cord is never broken,
We'll be true friends forever.

Don't kiss your sweetheart by the gate.
Love is blind, but the neighbors ain't.

I never went to college,
I never went to school.
But when it comes to lovin'
I'm an educated fool.

Billy gave me apples
Billy gave me pears,
Billy gave me fifteen cents
And kissed me on the stairs.

Love is like a mountain lizard.
It slides down your throat
And nibbles at you gizzard.

Columbus discovered America
In 1492.
But I discovered something better
When I discovered you.

The ocean is wide
And I can't step it.
I love you
And you can't help it.

State of love
Date of wishes
18 hugs
41 kisses.

No one saw me
No one knows
That I kissed you
On the tip of your nose.

One old hen
And ten little chickens.
I love you
To beat the dickens.

God made man
As fair as a BUBBLE.
Man made love
And love made TROUBLE.

Max Decker, Ed. D.

Kiss me quick
Kiss me cunning
Kiss me quick
For Ma is coming.

When you fall in a river,
There is a boat.
When you fall in a well,
There is a rope.
When you fall in love,
There is no hope.

If I had all the gold
That rolls across the sea,
I'd give it all and think it small
To know that you loved me.

I love coffee.
I love tea.
I love the boys
And they love me.

Do you love me?
Do you not?
You told me once
But I forgot.

Love is like an onion
We taste it with great delight.
But when it is gone we wonder
What even made us bite.

Love is love
But oh how sad
To love a girl
With a cross old dad.

Remember the pigeon
Remember the dove
Remember the night
We fell in love.

A ring is round
And has no end
So is my love
For you, my friend.

Some say it is a sin to love.
I never asked the reason why
Cause if it is a sin for loving you,
I'll sin until I die.

Marriage

When you get married
And your old man gets cross,
Pick up the broom
And show him who is boss.

When you get married
And growing old
Your friends forsake you,
Your heart turns cold,
Your flour bin is empty
Your husband in debt
Think of me happy
As an old maid yet.

When you are married
And living at your ease,
Remember I am single
And doing as I please.

<u>Courtship</u>

The bark that is on a tree
Is awful tight.
When you squeeze a boy
Squeeze him with all your might.

I can live without friends
I can live without foes
But the girls in the country
Can't live without beaus.

The taller the tree,
The thicker the bark,
The younger the couple,
The sweeter they spark.

Tobacco is sweet
But, oh how bitter
To kiss the lips
Of a tobacco spitter.

Sugar is sweet.
Vinegar is sour.
When we meet,
We kiss for an hour.

Some kiss hot
Some kiss cold.
But some don't kiss
Until they are told.

Yours Till

Yours till bacon strips

Yours till the hens lay soft-boiled eggs

Yours till the catfish has kittens

Yours till the table wears stockings on its legs

Yours till dogwood barks

Yours till the Saturday Evening Post
Rides a Camel to Chesterfield
To see Old Gold
And makes a Lucky Strike

Yours till bobby pins
Get sick on the permanent wave

Yours till the ocean goes dry

Yours till the dresser
Comes downstairs
To change its drawers

Yours till the Mississippi
Wears rubber pants
To keep its bottom dry

Advice

Marry for love and not for riches.
Marry a man who will wash the dishes.

> Goodnight,
> Sleep tight,
> But don't let
> The bedbugs bite.

Underline: Wondering What to Write

    You ask me in your book to write
    But, oh, what will it be?
    How can I write my thoughts to one,
    I love as well as thee?

Underline: Remember Me

    Remember Grant
    Remember Lee
    To heck with them
    Remember ME.

    Remember me early
    Remember me late
    Remember me as your
    Old school mate.

    When far away and out of sight,
    Remember me by what I write.
    And if the grave shall be my bed,
    Remember me when I am dead.

    Remember me long
    Remember me ever
    Remember the fun we had together.

    What shall I write?
    What shall it be?
    Just two little words--
    REMEMBER ME.

    Remember the old school days
    When we were young?
    We pulled each other's hair
    And chewed each other's gum.

Writers' Situation

>I thunk, I thunk
>I thunk in vain,
>I thunk by jinks
>I'd sign my name.

Friendship

>Money can't buy it.
>It is never for sale;
>One is bankrupt without it,
>With it you can't fail.
>It grows as it ages,
>And you should agree
>That our friendship is priceless
>To both you and me.
>
>There is room for me in your autograph.
>There is room for me in your heart.
>There is room for us both in heaven
>Where true friends never part.

Games

The following games were played by classmates and me during the eight years we attended a one-room school and during the four years I taught in a one-room country school in the southern Ozarks not far from the Arkansas-Missouri border.

Games of Ozark children are among the most interesting aspects of the region's folklore. No one knows the number of different versions which originated among the children themselves. Often they made their own rules. If they did not like the way a game was played, they changed it to their liking. These games show the original creativeness of a young mind as they played the game and how many communities played the games in different ways. All the games had much activity such as running, jumping, yelling and singing.

Over the rocks and hills, which children had as their playground at the country school or at home, they chased and pushed and fell. But the skinned knees, the stone bruised heels, the stumped toes, the bleeding noses, the frost-bitten ears and the scratched legs made the games no less an enjoyment that helped develop their interest and occupied their time.

No one knows the value of these simple little games. But many would agree that despite the simplicity and the absence of play equipment, these games created a sound democratic atmosphere of fair play, leadership and respect for others which helped the boys and girls develop into men and women.

Slap Hands--The children who played this game formed a circle as they sat on the floor or ground. One person placed their hand on the floor or the ground. Then the other players stacked their hands on top. The hand on the bottom was pulled out rapidly and placed on top of the other hands. This was repeated until the hands were going so fast that they were completely out of place. The winner was the player who had their hand on top after all others had stopped. This was a game that could be played inside if it was raining or showing.

Shinny--Children chose sides and hit a tin can with a stick to see which side could destroy the can or keep it going the longest.

At the country school it was difficult to control the can since the ground was seldom level. Rocks, mounds of dirt and ditches got in the way. It was also difficult to have a can all the time since few people bought anything in a tin can at the local country store. So destroying the can was not practiced often.

Hide the Thimble--One child was chosen to hide the thimble while others hid their eyes. After the thimble was hidden, the other players hunted for it. The one who found it did the hiding the next time. This went on until everyone was ready to start a different game. If they did not have a thimble, they used a small rock, a marble or a piece of wood. To help the hunters, the one who hid the thimble gave hints of the location by saying "Hot" if they were getting close to the hiding place or they said "Cold" if they were getting too far away.

Drop the Handkerchief--All players formed a circle and held their hands out behind them. The person who was chosen as "it" went slowly around the circle several times. Suddenly the "it" dropped the handkerchief in someone's hand. The "it" usually dropped the handkerchief in the hands of someone they thought they could out-run or in the hands of someone they liked. For example, a boy might have dropped the handkerchief in the hands of a girl he liked. This let her know that she was gaining his attention. After the drop the person who had the handkerchief ran after the person who dropped it. If the person who dropped it got around to the open place in the circle before the one with the handkerchief, the one with the handkerchief was "it" and the game went on. Children liked to use a red handkerchief, but if no one had one, any color would do.

Stink Base--The players formed two lines with the same number of players on each line. The two lines were about fifty to one hundred yards apart. This distance was determined by the players. Everyone from one line went over to the other and dared to be chased. If a player was caught, they were taken to an area called the "Stink Base". There they were guarded by players designated as guards. The side which lost the player tried to steal the person from the base by touching their hand. But if they were touched by a guard, they became a prisoner and went to the "Stink Base". The side which had the most players on their base was the winner. The end of the game was determined when the bell rang indicating that recess was over or when the players decided they wanted to start a new game.

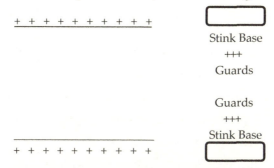

Hull Gull--This game was usually played with grains of corn or marbles. Two people usually played together. One player put marbles or grains of corn in their hand and said "Hull Gull. Hand full. How many?" The other players tried to guess the number of marbles or grains of corn. If they guessed the correct number, they got what was in the player's hand. If they guessed incorrectly, they had to give the other player the number of marbles or grains of corn they had in their hand. The player who got all the grains of corn or marbles was the winner.

Horn Horn--This game was played by several children. One was chosen as the leader. As the leader named animals, the players listened for the name of animals with horns. When such an animal was named, the player would say "Horn Horn" and win a point. If an animal that had horns was named and no one said "Horn Horn" the leader got a score. The player with the most points at the end of the game was the winner. The game lasted as long as the players wanted to play.

Sheep in My Pen--This game was played by a large group of children. One person was "it" and the other players ran and hid as the "it" counted to one hundred. If the person who was "it" saw someone, they yelled "Sheep in my pen," and that person came to the pen which was a circle drawn in the dirt. The only way that a player could get out of the pen was to get a wave from another player who was hiding. So they yelled "Give me a wave. Give me a wave," until they got one. But if the "it" saw the player giving the wave, they yelled "Sheep in my pen" and that player had to come to the pen. The game went on until all players were in the pen or until everyone agreed to stop the game.

Bluffman--An equal number of players stood in two rows about fifty feet apart. The "it" stood on a "bluff" which was a mound of dirt between the two lines and yelled "Bluffman." Then all the players ran until they reached the opposite side. While the players were running, the Bluffman tried to catch them. Those who were caught stayed on the "Bluff" and helped catch the others as the game went on. The "Bluffman" won when all the players were on the "Bluff." Each side could win if they had the fewest players on the "Bluff."

Pig in My Pen--"Pig in My Pen" was similar to "Sheep in My Pen." A circle was drawn in the dirt. Inside the circle the keeper stood guarding his pigs. The keeper had been chosen by the players. While the keeper shut their eyes, the other players ran and hid. If the keeper saw anyone, he yelled "Pig in my pen," and that person had to come to the circle. Those that were caught yelled "Pig wants a motion," and looked for someone. If they got a motion or wave, they went and hid again. The game went on until everyone was in the pen or until everyone agreed to start a new game.

There is also a folksong called "Pig in the Pen."

Wolf Over the Ridge--Players formed two lines about fifty yards apart. One side yelled "Wolf over the ridge," and the other side yelled "What will you have?" The answer was "A big fat lamb," and the others yelled "Catch me if you can." At this moment they began to run to catch the players from the other side before they got back to their line. If they were caught, they became members of the other group. This continued until one side had all the players.

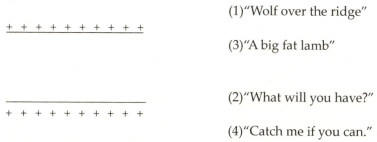

(1)"Wolf over the ridge"

(3)"A big fat lamb"

(2)"What will you have?"

(4)"Catch me if you can."

Two Deep--This game was similar to "Drop the Handkerchief." Players formed a circle in couples, one standing behind the other. Two players who were "it" began chasing each other around the circle. If the person who was being chased stopped in front of a couple, the person behind or the third person standing began to run until they decided to stop in front of another couple. The game continued until someone wanted to play another game.

Tag--Tag was a free-for-all type game. The players ran everywhere. There was no formation, no lines. The players just gathered in a group, elected an "it" and at the count of ten by the "it" they began to run. If the "it" caught or touched someone, they became the "it" and ran and chased until they caught someone. The players just ran everywhere to avoid getting touched by the "it" or caught by the "it".

Sometimes they included in the rules that if the "it" touched someone on the knee, for example, the new "it" must hold their hand on the knee as they chased other players.

Often the game of "Tag" became an I-CAN-OUTRUN-YOU game and the players ran as hard as they could to show others they had the ability to outrun someone.

<u>Wood Tag</u>--"Wood Tag" was similar to just plain "Tag". It was played by many children. One person, chosen as the "it" tried to catch other players before they could find any type of wood to touch. They were safe as long as they held to the piece of wood. If someone was caught who was not touching wood, they became the "it" and tried to catch someone. The game had no end. It just continued until the players were ready to start a new game.

<u>Ante-Over</u>--"Ante-Over" was played by any number of children. A rubber ball about the size of a softball was used. One-half of the players got on one side of the school building and one-half got on the other side. One side got the ball and threw it over the schoolhouse yelling "Ante-Over" as they threw the ball. If no one on the other side caught the ball, they threw the ball back. But if they caught the ball, they came around the schoolhouse and tried to hit someone with the ball. The person they hit came over to be a member of their side.

Usually the players established rules which said that a ball must bounce down the roof of the building or not go beyond a certain mark they had made or they would yell "FOUL" and the ball would be thrown again. This prevented a large, strong player from throwing the ball too high or too far so no one would have a chance to catch it.

<u>New Orleans</u>--"New Orleans" was similar to "Stink Base" except the words or calls were different. The players

formed two lines with the same number of players in each line. The lines were approximately fifty to one hundred yards apart. Everyone from one line went over close to the other line as possible and the following conversation went on: "Where are you from"? The other side answered "New Orleans." The players who had challenged the other side said "What do you have"? Then they added "Show me if you can." The players being challenged made signs with their hands, arms, mouths or entire body. If the challengers could guess what they had, they selected one of their players and returned to their line. Then the other challengers on the other side did the same thing. The side game was the winner.

Wave--One player was "it". Others hid as the "it" counted to fifty. After they had hidden, the "it" tried to find them. If the "it" saw them, they yelled their name and the player had to come to the circle drawn in the dirt. Before they could hide again, they had to get a wave from another player. Then they had to slip away without the "it" seeing them. If they were caught leaving the circle, they had to return and get another wave.

Spin the Bottle--A group of players gathered on the floor or ground. One player who was the "it" spun a bottle. When it stopped, the neck of the bottle would point to one player. Then the person who was "it" got to have this person do anything they wished. After the player had done what was asked of them, they spun the bottle and the game went on.

Mother, May I--Any number of players formed a line. One player who was the "it" stood about fifty feet in front of the other. They told the others what to do. For example, the "it" might have told one player to take two elephant steps or one rabbit step. However, if the player who was told to take a step did not say "Mother, May I" they had to go back to the line and start over again. The player who reached the line where the "it" was standing was the winner. Players could slip forward carefully if the leader did not see them. But if they were caught, they were sent back to start over again.

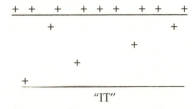

Pleased or Displeased--Any number of players could play this game. One person acted as the leader and asked other players if they were "pleased or displeased." If the player said they were pleased, the leader went on to another player. If the player said they were displeased, they were asked what it would take to please them. They may have said that they wanted someone to hug another person's neck; they might have wanted someone to walk on their knees across the room. After they were granted their wish, they were considered pleased and the leader went on to the next player.

Red Rover--Children formed two lines about fifty feet apart. Those in each line held hands. One line invited a member of the other group to run toward their line and attempt to break through. They yelled, "Red Rover. Red Rover. Come over. Come over." If the player could not break through the line, they had to become a member of that side. If they were able to break through, they could select a player to take back with them to their side. The side with the most players at the end of the game was the winner.

Tap the Rabbit--Children at rural one-room schools liked to play this game. They joined hands and formed a circle. One boy and one girl joined hands and walked around the outside of the circle. They were the "it". Soon they tapped the hands of another couple. Then each couple ran in the opposite direction. The couple that reached the gap in the line left by the tapped couple was the winner. The couple that did not get back first had to continue to tap some other couple until they won a race and got back in the circle.

The "it" couple ran counter clockwise after they made their tap and the tapped couple ran clockwise. Sometimes they would almost collide as they went around the circle. Some ran so fast that they stumbled and fell down on the rough ground but they got up immediately and continued the run. They wanted to show the other two and the rest of the students in the circle that they had the ability to run fast and that a fall would not stop them.

The only sounds that came from this game were the yells for some couple as they tried to beat someone else back to the gap in the line. Other children in the line who were not running seemed to have favorites and yelled for their couple. But the competition was friendly and no one ever seemed to get mad or get their feelings hurt. As in most of the games they developed their own rules and everyone played by them.

<u>Goul Down</u>--This game was played by any number of children. One person was the leader. The leader threw a stick. The other players ran and hid while the leader ran to get the stick. He brought it back to the base. When the leader saw a player, they ran, held on to the stick and yelled "Goul Down," and called the name of the player they had seen. If someone would slip to the base and throw the stick without getting caught, the players on the base who had been caught ran and hid again while the poor leader went after the stick.

Rounder--This game was similar to softball except the players worked their way from left field to bat. For example, the left fielder went to center field when an out was made. The center fielder went to right field and the right fielder went to third base. The third baseman went to short stop; the short stop went to second base; the second baseman went to first base; the first baseman became pitcher; the pitcher became the catcher and the catcher came to bat. The player who made the out went to left field and started all over again on their way to bat. Children played hard to get an out for everyone was anxious to become batter. This was an individual game but it was a cooperative game as they tried to get someone out.

Board on Deck--This was a ball game played with a rubber ball about the size of a baseball. Two sides were formed. One side went to the field and the other side to bat. There was a pitcher, catcher, batters, a guard at each deck and as many fielders as they wanted. If a batter got three strikes, they were out. The game went on for any length of time. When a batter was walked, four balls, they went on the first deck. When a batter hit a ball, they might touch the first deck and run to the second deck. If they hit the ball hard enough, they might run to second deck and back to first. This counted as a score. But it was difficult to do this because there were boundaries set beyond which the ball could not go. If the ball was hit beyond these boundaries, it was an out. This made it impossible for a large, strong player to dominate the game. If the batter hit the ball but was unable to run to the second deck, they would go to the first deck and run to the second if the next batter hit a good ball or if they were able to steal a run to the second deck or from the second deck back to the first. Most cuts were made when any person in the field hit a player running from one deck to the other with the soft rubber ball. Or the catcher might see someone off the first deck and throw the ball at them or the pitcher might through the ball to any fielder who might have an easy shot at a runner. The object of the game was to score as many points as possible before the other side got three outs.

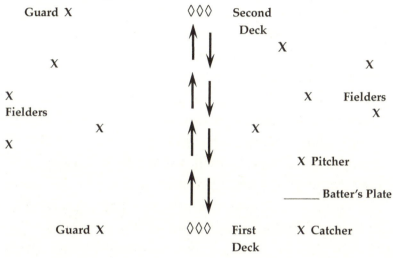

Geography Match--A favorite game at the country school on Friday after the last recess was "Geography Match". Each child had a geography book with the same map. The leader or teacher would place the first location to be found on the chalkboard. For example, B----N was placed on the board and everyone would search for such a word on the map. When someone found BOSTON, they got a score and were allowed to write a location on the board. The player who got the most scores was the winner. As the game progressed, more difficult names were placed on the board:

B----K, BISMARCK, C---R, CASPER, L---G, LANSING, D-- M----S R---R, DES MOINES RIVER, H-S, HAYS or B---E, BOISE.

Students learned much place geography from this game. They learned the location and names of states, towns, mountains and rivers. Sometimes they would play the game with one country or a continent. Often the children changed the rules or made new ones. Sometimes, if a student found the correct place but did not pronounce it correctly, they did not get a score. Often, they made a rule that required the player who found Bismarck, for example, had to pronounce it correctly, tell what state it was in and in what part of the state it was located.

<u>Cipher</u>--"Cipher" was a game involving arithmetic. Two sides were chosen. The first name on one side would cipher with the first name on the other side. Someone, usually the teacher would give a problem like 4,441 multiplied by 121. The first player to work the problem and read the answer was the winner, if it was correct, and got a score. The winner then faced the second name on the other side. The winner was allowed to select the type of problem which they wished to be given. If the winner was good at long division, they would select that type of problem. If they knew that the person against whom they were ciphering was not so good at a certain type of problem, they would select such a problem. Sometimes the first name on one side would "turn down" all of the players on the other side. This was why it was important to select the best person in arithmetic first on each side. Addition, subtraction, multiplication, division, and fractions were the type of problem most often chosen. Players were not only required to work the problem correctly, read the answer first but also their work on the chalkboard had to be readable and understandable by the teacher. No steps in working the problem could be left out. Many students became fast in

working problems and learned many arithmetic basics as they worked hard problems and enjoyed the competition.

Fox and Geese--In this game one player was the fox and the other players were the geese. The geese ran into the woods and hid. However, they had to leave a trail for the fox. The trail that they left was tiny bits of paper. The fox followed the trail until it found the geese. Then the fox had to run as fast as possible back to the base and yell that the geese had been found. From then on the players took turns being the fox.

There is also a board game called "Fox and Geese."

King of the Mountain--In this game several players climbed on a mound of dirt, a sawdust pile or a haystack. Another group of players attacked the players on the mound and tried to throw them off. The player who stayed on the longest was "King of the Mountain." This was a rough game and many rural teachers would not allow the students to play it.

Red Line--In this game the players divided into groups. Each group got behind a line they had drawn in the dirt. The two lines were about thirty feet apart. Each side tried to get the other players to come as close to their line as possible. When they got close, the other side tried to catch a player. If a player was caught, they went to the other side. The winner was the side with the most players at the end of the game.

Fruit Basket--Players formed a circle and the person chosen as "it" went around naming each player the name of a fruit. The "it" went to the center of the circle and called the name of a fruit three times. If the player who was that fruit did not yell the name of the fruit before the "it" finished, they had to go to the center and become the "it". At certain times the "it" yelled the words, "Fruit Basket

Turned Over." When they did this, everyone changed seats with another player and changed fruits with the player whose seat they got. If someone did not find a seat or did not remember the name of the new fruit they were to have, they became the "it".

Laugh and Go Foot--In this game two lines were formed with boys on one side and girls on the other. They held hands. Some player went down the line and told the boys a question to ask the girls. Example: What does your father say 'bout boys? Another player went down the line and told each girl an answer. Example: They are no good skunks. The boy asked the question three times. The girl answered three times. They had to do this without laughing. If they laughed, they went to the foot of the line and started all over again. This game was played by school children but adults also played the game at parties they had. This was a fun game because sometimes the questions and answers became strange and ridiculous.

Bluejay--This was a party game for older children. It was played at night at play parties. A boy and a girl stood in the dark about fifty yards from the other players. When the girl called the name of another girl, the girl began to run in the direction of the caller. Soon after the girl's name was called, the boy called the name of a boy. This boy tried to catch the girl and yell "Bluejay" before the girl got to the finish line. If the boy caught the girl, he got to kiss her. In most cases the girl did not run very fast.

Tumblebug Wager--Tumblebugs are beetles. Sometimes they are scavengers. Sometimes they are called dung beetles because they roll together a perfectly round ball of dung, bury it and lay their eggs in it. Most children believed the bugs were working together as they rolled the ball of dung to the place where they would bury it. There seemed to be complete cooperation between the two bugs so children often called them such names as Tom Puller and John Pusher. However some experts said that one was trying to steal the ball from the other.

Children enjoyed the actions of this "bug" and didn't mind the smell. They would bet two marbles, for example, that the "bugs" would take their ball south. Others would bet north or east or west. Whoever won got everyone's marbles. The game went on for hours because the bugs moved slowly.

The Snake Game--If one wanted to test their skill at running fast, they could find a Blue Racer snake. All they had to do was to provoke one or two and the race was on. Most people believed that they would not bite you but they liked to chase you. But you could run for awhile and stop and the snakes would stop but most everyone agreed that a person could not out-run one. School children, usually boys, would bet a marble that one of them could out-run the snake. This was an exciting game. They were just a little afraid of the snake and they wanted to get the other person's marble. So they ran as fast as they could.

The Doodlebug Game--Children and even some adults got much enjoyment from watching Doodlebugs or Ant Lions in their hill. These interesting bugs built small pits in the soft dirt. Much of the time the bug could not be seen but the dirt which made the pit would move slightly now and then letting the watcher know that the bug was there. If an ant came by not looking where they were going and fell into the pit, it was soon killed by the Doodlebug. Children took turns watching these hills and put their mouths close to the pit and said "Doodlebug come out of your pit. Doodlebug, doodlebug where have you been? Doodlebug, doodlebug let me see your head again. Doodlebug, doodlebug come out of your pit." The first one who saw the bug in the bottom of the pit was the winner of the game.

<u>Stick Horses</u>--Children would cut a stick about four or five feet long and "play like it was a horse. They would put it between their legs and run and gallop for hours. If they wanted a certain color of horse, they selected the wood they needed and left the bark on it. For example, a sycamore stick was a good white horse. White oak was perfect for a dapple-gray. Black oak or black jack was used for black horses and sassafras made a good sorrel.

<u>Horseshoes</u>--Both children and adults liked to play horseshoes. The object of the game was to throw two horseshoes about forty feet, the distance varied from community to community, and get as close to a stake as possible. Or better yet throw the shoe around the stake, which counted five points. This was called a ringer. Or a leaner was not bad. If the shoe leaned against the stake, it counted three points. The second player tried to get their shoes closer to the stake or they tried to knock a leaner down or hit the ringer and knock it off or if they could "cap" it with their own ringer, the first ringer did not count. The player who had their shoes closest to the stake got two points if both of their shoes were closer.

Then the players at the other end threw their shoes and tried to do the same thing as the first two players.

The first two players to reach a score of twenty-one were the winners and the losers had to "sit-out" until their time came around again.

<u>Marbles</u>--In the Ozarks during the days of one-room schools, marbles were a prized possession of boys and girls. Almost every boy and girl had a sack of marbles that they carried just in case someone wanted to play a game.

They were made in many different colors. Some were

Max Decker, Ed. D.

red and white swirls; some were solid green, blue or yellow. Many were striped with brilliant colors.

Several games were played with marbles. Some of the games were handed down from other generations and many were created by the children for they had a knack for creativity. They liked to make their own rules so from one place to another the rules might be different. But when a rule was made at a school or in a community, they stuck to it religiously, unless a majority voted to change it.

At the beginning of a game the players decided if they would play for fun or play for "keeps." If they were playing for "keeps," they got to keep all the marbles they hit with the taw, according to the rules of the game. Most teachers in one-room country schools frowned on the game "for keeps" because they considered it gambling, but it went on anyway.

A taw was a large marble used for shooting and hitting other marbles. A good taw was good to have.

The following are examples of the most popular marble games played in the Ozarks: It should be noted that the diagrams of holes, lines and circles are drawn to correspond with how they looked dug or drawn in the dirt.

Game 1

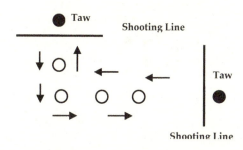

To play this game of marbles, four holes were dug in the ground. They were about two inches deep. The rocks and rough places between the holes were cleaned and smoothed as best they could be. Still they were rather rough at first. The object of this game was to take the taw or any sized marble the players chose, shoot from the starting line and try to get the marble in the first hole. If they made it into the first hole, they would try to get in the second hole. If they could get the marble in all four holes, they could go to the end starting line and go back toward the first hole. If they made it back to the first hole, they were the winner. But this was difficult to do unless they were expert shooters. But there was danger if they missed a hole. The next player could shoot at the first player's marble if they got into the hole closest to the marble. If they hit the first player's marble, the first player had to start over.

The second player could go on to the next hole after they hit the first player's marble. Sometimes, if they had agreed to use small marbles, they were allowed to use a larger marble, the taw, to shoot at the other player's marble.

Game 2

Another game was played like the diagram below on the right. The players drew a rather large circle in the ground, usually with a stick, and placed twelve marbles inside the circle.

The object of this game was to knock a marble out of the circle with their taw. If they were able to do that, they got another shot and got to keep the marble. The rules of the game that were made before the game started usually said that a player could knock

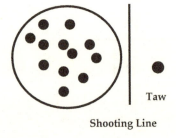

Taw

Shooting Line

only one marble out of the circle at a time. If the first player did not get the marble out, the second player tried to do the same thing. The player with the most marbles after all were out of the circle was the winner. If they were playing for fun, they took the marbles that belonged to them. If they were playing "for keeps" they kept the marbles that they had knocked out of the circle.

<u>Game 3</u>

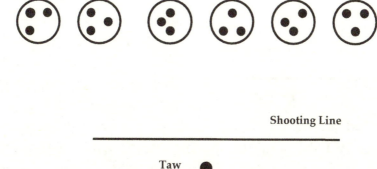

Shooting Line
_____

Taw ●

In this game the first player shot from the shooting line, which was two or three feet away, with his taw. The player could select any circle to aim at and could knock out as many marbles as possible. When a player completed one circle, they could start on another.

When the first player failed to get a marble out of the circle, the second player tried the same thing.

The winner was the one with the most marbles after all were out of all the circles.

<u>Game 4</u>

In this game a large circle was drawn in the dirt and one marble was placed in the center. The object was to knock the marble out with

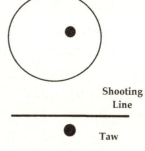

the taw. The first player to get the marble out was the winner. A player had to be careful and not leave the marble too close to the line for that would make it easier for the next player to get it out. The shooting line was two or three feet from the circle, depending on the rules established before the game.

Game 5

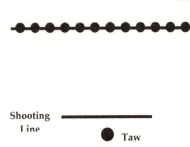

This game was played as follows: The first player, using a taw or smaller marble, shot from the shooting line at a marble they selected. If they hit the marble, they kept it and selected another and shot until they missed. The second player did the same thing. The player who hit the most marbles was the winner. At times the rules were relaxed some and a player could just shoot and hit any marble.

Game 6

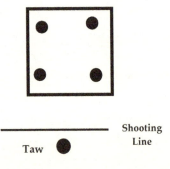

The square design drawn in the dirt contained four marbles. The first player had to shoot at the marbles clockwise around the square and knock the marbles out of the square. If they missed, the second player did the same thing. The first player to get the last marble out of the square was the winner.

In most marble games two players played but any number could play. These were the six games that were most popular. However, children created many other marble games and had fun playing. Some of the other game designs and rules will follow.

Most players held the shooting marble between the thumb and the trigger finger. The thumb was the most important finger to a good shooter.

Other games, in addition to the popular six are as follows:

Game 7

In this game the marbles were staggered along two lines. The rules were to hit the marble nearest the shooting line first and go as far as possible. If a player missed a marble, the next player got to start their shooting. The player, who hit the most marbles before all were gone, was the winner.

Game 8

This marble game was played with fifteen marbles. Nine marbles of the same color were placed in a line about one foot apart. Three marbles were placed at various spots, three on each side of the line, about two feet from those in the line. The first player shot his taw at the first marble in the line. If they were able to hit all the marbles in the line with nine shots, they started

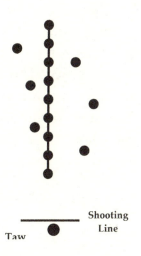

back toward the starting line, shooting at the closest marble to them. At any time they missed a marble, the next player got their turn to shoot. At the end of the game, the winner was the one who had hit the most marbles.

Game 9

This game was played with fifteen marbles. The first player shot their taw from the shooting line but they had to shoot at the marble at the end of the line and work their way back to the first marble. If the player missed a marble, the next player got to shoot. If any player hit a marble not in the line of rotation, they lost their turn and all the marbles they had hit. The player with the most marbles at the end of the game was the winner.

Game 10

This game looked simple but it was difficult. The players had to hit the marbles from left to right and knock them into the second space. The marble 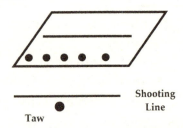 hit could not touch any line. When a player hit a marble that touched a line after its roll, the next player got to shoot. The player who got the most of the five marbles in the second space was the winner.

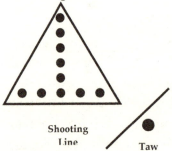

Game 11

This marble game was played with ten marbles. The player shot from an angle as indicated in the diagram. Each marble had to be knocked out of the lines. The player had to begin with the right-hand marble on the bottom row, go across, then shoot at the first marble and go up the line of marbles in order. Any marble hit by the player out of this order caused the player to forfeit a shot and loose all the marbles he had collected. The winner was the player with the most marbles at the end of the game.

Game 12

The kite design game was played with twelve marbles. All shooting had to be done from the shooting line. The marbles had to be hit in rotation from the nearest one to the one at the top of the kite. The marbles on the tail of the kite only had to be hit.

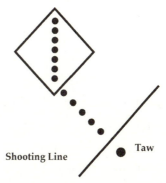

Those within the kite had to be knocked out of the lines. The marbles hit were not collected by the player. Instead, hitting a marble on the tail of the kite counted one point. Hitting a marble from the kite design counted three points. The winner was the player who had the most points after all marbles had been hit or knocked out of the kite.

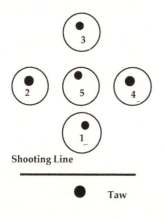

Game 13

The players in this game had to shoot at the marble in circle number one, first, and knock it out of the circle. If they did this, they could go on to marble number two and go on until they missed. When they missed, the second player could shoot. The player with the most marbles won.

Choosing-Up

Choosing-Up was not a game but it was necessary to do for many games that had two sides. Choosing who would be on one side or the other was a delicate process. Children wanted to win and they wanted to have friends on their side. So sometimes friendship won over power and skill. Sometimes power and skill won.

Two students, usually eighth graders in a one-room country school, would take it upon themselves to be the "its" for each side. Then they would do something to see who got the first selection. Most of the time they took a stick or a baseball bat, if they had one, and placed their hand where they caught the bat thrown to them by the other it. Then the other player would place their hand in a grasp position above the other player's hand. This went on until they reached the top of the stick and had a complete grasp on the stick. Then they had to throw the stick over their head backward at least ten feet. If they did this, they got the first pick of a player to be on their side. Often a student who was not good at the game or who was not popular was left until last.

Choosing-Up brought a good self-image for some but not for others. I have seen players who were chosen last every time. I know they must have felt left-out and probably did not enjoy the game as they should have.

Chapter 5

Folksay

Folks did say what they pleased and how they pleased in the Ozarks. Yet, the pet sayings, exaggerations, strange comparisons, and by-words served their purpose and got the idea across. Some people used "cuss" words as they talked. Some people thought they did this because they didn't have a very large vocabulary so they just used these words as fillers. All people of this area did not use the hill language but those who did were not concerned about any "high falutin ways of talking that did not make sense."

<u>Sayings</u>
  Sayings were a part of the everyday language of people in this area. Even though many of them were not correct grammar, they did add color, humor and wit to the conversations. And they did help people get their point across if they were talking to another person of the area.
  These ways of talking may have been in the form of statements such as "Something is dead up the branch." This meant that something strange was going on. All statements meant something as they were woven into the conversations of the people. The following is a list of sayings that have been used in this area for several generations:

- My nose runs and my feet smell. (The person is feeling badly).
- We laid back our ears and went after it. (We ate like we had not eaten in a month).
- Even a blind sow finds an acorn once in awhile. (Everyone has some luck now and then).
- Lost his marbles. (Someone has lost his mind or is acting crazy).
- Cutting a new path. (A boy was late to a party. His dad said he supposed he was cutting a new path or going in a different direction or getting there a different way).
- Put that on the back burner. (Wait awhile or do it later).
- I could eat a sow and pigs and chase a boar for a quarter. (I am hungry).
- It will never be noticed on a galloping horse. (No one will ever notice something about or on anyone who moves around).
- That will make him chew his rosin. (That will make him think or change his actions).
- No use to have a wagon unless you have a load to hall. (You don't have to have something big or expensive if your job is small).
- Antigoglin. (Not straight across. Cutting across making the distance shorter).
- He has enough money to burn a wet mule. (The person has plenty of money).
- They don't have a pot to piss in or a window to throw it out of. (A person who is very poor).
- They had about as much chance as a snowball in hell. (They did not have much of a chance to get something done).
- He's been cuckolded. (A man's wife has been unfaithful to him).

- She's off her rocker. (She's crazy).
- Catawampus. (Crooked, out of line not as it should be).
- Darn your hide. (A mild disapproval).
- Cagey as a peach orchard boar. (A person is tricky, cunning or sexy).
- Tanked (Drunk—The effects of moonshine or any liquor).
- "I don't want me no fat man, I want a tall man as long, slim and slick as a sycamore saplin." (What women say when they are looking for a man).
- Grass Widder. (A divorcee).
- Cut a fit. (Reacted to something in an exaggerated way. They may have cried, screamed or yelled).
- Young Sprouts. (Young people in their teens).
- When there is snow on the mountain, there is fire in the valley. (A man who has white hair may be very active sexually).
- The older the buck, the stiffer the horn. (An older man may be very active sexually).
- As useless as a one-legged man at an ass kickin. (Useless).
- It is a dusty road. (It is hard to see into the future).
- "Stinkin" mess. (A very bad situation).
- Itchy trigger finger. (Wanting to start a fuss).
- A cocked gun. (High temper. Ready to get mad or upset).
- Lose your shirt and all its fixtures. (When something happens that makes the economy uneasy or a person takes quite a financial risk they may "Lose their shirt and all its fixtures").
- He's not playin' with a full deck. (His mind is not working just right).

- KINGS-X. (When a child was playing a game like "tag" and they were tired and about to be caught, they could say KINGS-X and no one could touch them).
- Stands out like a wart on a billy goat's navel. (Something about you will be easy to detect or noticed by other people).
- You can shear a sheep as many times as you want to but you can only skin him once. (You can't fool an Ozarker all the time).
- There are lots of ways to kill a cat without choking it to death. (There are many ways to get things done in the Ozarks).
- Buy them for ten cents and sell them for a dollar. (Buy a person for what they are worth and sell them for what they think they are worth).
- Nervous as a whore in church. (A very nervous person).
- Three bricks short of a load. (A person who is not real bright).
- One bubble short of level. (Not functioning well mentally).
- They will "sashay" out of here. (To stroll this way and that way).
- Loosen up a cold. (A cough becomes less tight).
- They got sore at someone. (They got mad at someone).
- As ugly as a mud fence. (Someone who is very ugly).
- They would tear out the bone. (Some who worked hard and fast).
- They high-tailed it out of there. (They left in a hurry).
- It is a wonder she didn't fade into a swoon. (To become very excited).
- I haven't seen hide nor hair of them. (A missing person).
- Water won't run uphill. (Something that can't be done).

- She's hot to trot. (A woman who is ready to make love to just about any man).
- He wants everything that "jines" him. (A greedy farmer who wants everything around him).
- They will eat your breakfast. (Someone will "get the best" of you in some way).
- Don't that beat a hog a-flyin. (Something that is not expected to happen).
- Can't get over a bolster. (He is not much of a man who can't get over a pillow like that).
- Don't get down-wind from them. (They don't smell good).
- He smells as bad as a nest of young owls. (He doesn't smell good).
- They are pickin' on me. (Someone or several people are giving them a bad time).
- He is just like a crow. All he can do is holler, eat and shit. (A no-good man).
- They "saikoed" around. (Hill people who just walk around slowly acting like they are in no hurry).
- Won't last until the bread gets done. (Something that people in the Ozarks don't believe will last very long, like a marriage).
- Hop to it. (Go ahead and do something now if you want to).
- Here dreckly. (I will do this or that before long or as soon as I can get to it, or when I want to do it).
- First one thing, then another. (Doing several things).
- Butter done slipped off his/her biscuit. (Their mind is not working just right).
- You hit the nail on the head. (You got it right).

- The big coon is walkin' the log today. (When a very important person or a person who thought they were very important were, or seemed to be in charge).
- Tuckered Out. (A person who is very tired).
- Out-And-About. (Someone went someplace or away from home).
- If this book starts to roam, slap its face and send it home. (If you borrow a book, send it back to the owner).
- Ram Rod. (A person who pushed other people to get something done, usually their way).
- Son-Of-A-Gun. (An expression used in the Ozarks that means astonishment or disgust).
- Let's tighten our belts. (An expression used when people decide not to spend so much or make do with what they have for awhile).
- Feelin' their oats. (If someone seemed to be very happy and laughing more than usual or talking a lot).
- Slapdab. (A word used in the hills to mean the exact spot or place. Example: Slapdab in the middle).
- He can't hear himself "fart" in a jug. (Hard of hearing).
- Don't feel rained on. (Don't feel that you have got a bad deal).
- Gentleman gloggery I'm tanked. (They were drunk).
- For goodness sake. (Surprised or astonished).
- They waxed eloquent. (They talked correctly and effectively).
- Meetin' house. (A name for a church house where people went to worship)
- 2 Bits = .25 (Making change in the Ozarks).

  4 Bits = .50

  6 Bits = .75

  A DOLLAR
- The Last. (What the shoemaker used to kill his wife).

- That's on the other page. (That is a different subject. That is not what I am talking about).
- They just come one in a box like him. (He is different from anyone I know).
- He's not the only pebble on the beach. (He is not the only one).
- Six of one and a half dozen of the other. (There is no difference in the two).
- Raining pitch forks. (A very hard rain).
- O, shucks, Nancy, I can't dance. (I do not know how to do that).
- Cold enough to freeze the balls off a brass monkey. (Very cold).
- You can't make a silk purse out of a sow's ear. (You can't take something ordinary and make something splendid out of it).
- It's all down hill from here. (We have done the hardest part of our job. The rest will be easier).
- He's too big for his britches. (He acts like he can do anything but he is not capable of doing that).
- He puts his pants on the same way we all do. (He's no different or better than anyone else).
- Piss a blue streak. (To urinate well or do anything fast and well).

Bywords

Another form of saying was the byword that was thrown into a conversation about anywhere the person desired and as many times as they wanted to.
- By gosh, I found a dime.
- By grabs, I know when I'm drunk.
- Con found it, I lost my knife.
- By the eternal, I found it.

2 Soon 2 Be 4 Gotten

- Lords sake, that is a big snake.
- I de-clair, that snake came close to me.
- As the feller says, you never know where a snake will be.
- See, I by doggies, I nearly stepped on that snake.
- Shucks, I lost my pipe.
- Corn, that makes me mad.
- Dog my cats, I knew he would run.
- By thunder, my wife is goin' to have a little one.
- Goshins, it looks like a storm is coming.
- By Ned, I'm goin' to that dance tonight.
- By cracky, I believe in ghosts.
- By gingo, I shot that rabbit sixty feet away.
- By the way, I'm not that good a shot.
- Stars a livin', I never saw that many bats.
- I say, do you believe in the devil.
- My Lord, you can walk fast.
- Lord have mercy, I saw too much.
- Is that right? I know how it feels. Yes sir, right.
- Sure as shootin', I'll catch me a mess of fish.
- Right as right, I will tell my wife who is boss.
- Darn tootin', I ran when I saw that mountain lion.
- Dad gum, I mashed my finger.
- By gravy, we got her in a log.
- Fiddle sticks, I don't believe in ghosts.
- By grannies, I do know a man who is afraid of them.
- Dog gone, I have to leave now.
- Right Smart. The cow gives a right smart of milk.
- Jumpin' jack rabbits, that is loud thunder.
- Sam Hill, I knew that kid was his.
- Gimminey, that is rich milk.
- Gee, I'm gonna get out of here.
- Gee Whiz, I'm tired.

- Sakes alive, she don't expect that tonight!
- Heck fire, she can just let me take my time.
- Jimminy crickets. we are all in this together.
- I'll be. I wouldn't have thought that of her.
- You don't say. Well it was sure to happen.
- I knew it. She meant to marry him all the time.

Mispronunciations

Mispronunciations and strange word creations could be heard about any time. "Plumb" for entirely, "nat" for that, "catched" for caught, and "maters" for tomatoes were some good examples.

- Knowed for knew
- Shore for sure
- Dreckly for directly
- Hit for it
- Hoss for horse
- Ent for went
- Cumbers for cucumbers
- Oman for woman
- Et for eat or ate
- Clumb for climbed
- Niss for this

- Taters for potatoes
- This'n for this one
- Nather for neither
- Y for why
- Doo for dog
- Aurn for our own
- Outer for out of
- Offen for off of
- Offen for often
- Seed for saw

Comparisons

When people "have it in for someone" they didn't hesitate to let it be known and when they did voice their opinions, it might have been in the form of a comparison. The simile was used often. If their neighbor's dog kept them awake at night, the dog and the neighbor might have been spoken of "as worthless as an old shoe." However, if the neighbor corrected his dog and had dinner with the family, he and his dog were "as good as gold." Of course there were other words not listed here that neighbors used toward another neighbor, at times.

- Cold as blue blazes
- Sick as a blue bellied mule
- Thick as hair on a dog's back
- Thick as two in a bed
- Meaner than a rattlesnake
- Rougher than a cob
- Slick as a gut
- Slick as an eel
- Long as a fence rail
- Crooked as a snake
- Higher than the sky
- Sick as a pig
- Sicker than a mule
- Big as a cow
- Busy as a bee
- Quick as a cat
- As limber as a rag
- As low as a snake
- As red as a beet
- Tight as the bark on a tree
- Higher than a kite
- Blue as Ma's old coffee pot
- Green as grass
- Fresh as a daisy
- Happy as a lark
- Smooth as silk
- Slow as a snail
- Chipper as a chipmunk
- Big as a horse
- Sharp as a tack
- Quick as a wink
- Black as night
- Hot as fire
- Pretty as a picture
- Round as a pancake
- Jumpy as a frog
- Hungry as a bear
- Gentle as a lamb
- Cute as a bug's ear
- Crazy as a loon
- Green as a gourd
- Hollow as a log
- Cold as ice
- Slicker than a whistle
- Yeller than a punkin
- Dead as a doornail
- Sweet as honey
- Thick as fleas
- Full as a tick
- Wrinkled as a prune
- Wet as sop
- Dark as a dungeon
- Light as a feather
- Hard as a rock
- Wild as a buck
- Brown as a berry
- White as snow

- Soft as down
- Mean as the dickens
- Black as soot
- Cold as a wedge
- Blind as a bat
- Round as a butter biscuit
- Horny as a toad
- Old as the hills
- Frisky as a colt
- Right as rain
- Run like a scared rabbit
- Took off like a turpentined cat
- Eat like a horse
- Scream like a panther
- Clear as a bell
- Crooked as a dog's hind leg
- Straight as a string
- Hot as a firecracker
- Cold as a cucumber
- Skinny as a rail
- White as a sheet
- Wicked as a witch
- Tall as a pine
- Round as a dollar
- Sound as a dollar
- Clean as a hound's tooth
- Fuzzy as a peach
- Hotter than blue blazes
- Deep as a well
- Longer than my arm
- Lit up like a Christmas tree
- Silly as a pet coon
- Keen as a razor
- Red as blood
- Stiff as a poker
- Stupid as a goat
- Stubborn as a mule
- As calm as a clock
- As brisk as a bee
- Tall as a giant
- Big as a battleship
- Awkward as a cow
- Swims like a duck
- Nutty as a squirrel
- Ugly as sin
- As black as your hat
- As cold as a grave
- As easy as pie
- As nervous as a cat
- As scarce as hen's teeth
- Poor as Job's turkey
- Awkward as a bull in a china shop
- Black as the devil
- Grows like a weed
- Old fashioned as a flitter
- Quick as a whip
- Wild as an Indian
- Ugly as the day is long
- Mad as an old wet hen

- As poor as church mice
- Black as a crow
- As light as a feather
- Dumb as an ox
- As deep as the sea
- Fit as a fiddle
- Sour as kraut
- Blinkin' like a toad in a hailstorm
- Tight as a drum
- Dull as lead
- Run like a chicken with its head cut off
- Run like a cat with its tail on fire
- Fat as a butter ball
- Clear as mud
- Blue as the sky
- Strong as coffee
- Soft as a kitten
- Sweet as a baby
- Free as a bird
- Steep as a horse's face
- Slick as a minnow's lip
- As faithful as a dog
- As close as two peas in a pod
- Kick like a mule
- Faster than greased lightning
- Slow as ten year itch
- Pretty as a speckled pup
- Dry as a bone

Conversation

Conversation hit an enjoyable peak at social gatherings such as dinner-on-the-ground, pie suppers and at town on Saturday, not to mention what was said on the local telephone.

Most conversation was helped along by whole-hearted agreement on the part of the listener. While one person was talking, the listener kept a good feeling going by saying at frequent intervals: "Shore enough," Lands sake," "Oh, my," "Right," "That's right," "Hum," "Well, well," "Yes sir," "I knowed it," "I'll bet that is right," "You don't say," "I'll be darned," "Damned if I would," "You're right as can be," "I would, I would," "Hell no," "Gosh," "Shucks," and "Ain't that a sight."

Yet there was a great enjoyment gained by this. To talk was a treat. To listen was not bad but few did it.

The following are a few examples of such talk that could be heard as one went around the square of any small town on Saturdays in the Ozarks.

A hunter was telling about an animal his dogs had treed and said, "Hit clim' a tree, lept out and the dogs took arter. Hit clear ran clear off and left hit."

A man in the community was sick and several of the neighbors were at his house settin'-up with him. Along in the night one man said, "I do believe he needs an enema." Another feller who seemed to be in charge said, "Well, I think it would be all right but I don't believe he could ever swallow it."[5]

Uncle George, who was cross-eyed, said, "I tell you that are spring is a sight of a good un. Iven drunk outer of hit for years to come."

Another neighbor was sick. Uncle Jim asked Grandpa Scoonse if he was conscious. He answered, "Yeah, he's jist as conscious as he can be or ever will be until he is dead as he can be."

A man was talking about his wife knowing something that the others did not know. He said, "We tried and tried and finally got it outer in."

A man was over on the corner of a street talking to his neighbor. "The weather shore is bad, ain't it. I shore wish we could have a fair spell. Believe it would help my bones."

Two fox hunters were telling about the night before when their dogs did a wonderful job. "I'll tell you, Ole Drum was a dandy. Did you see him hit the trail under that big sycamore tree? I bet that dog never smelt anything better in his life.

"But that bitch never would take holt. She jist ran around tryin' to find them damn rabbits or after that dog that was hot on that fox. I'll sell that bitch for ten dollars the first time I get a chance. I'll not have a dog around to disgrace me. But I bet you ain't got no dog around that can stay with Ole Drum. Know damb well you ain't. Not any dog in this country that can or ever could uncover as many leaves as that dog unless it was Ole Singer that my dad owned when I was a lad. That was a dog if I ever saw one. Could smell for over a mile against the wind."

Grandma Muscoo was having health problems. "I'm all stove up. Them leaders in my legs hurt mighty bad. My head hurts and my kidneys ain't actin' right. I'm just all in."

Place Names

Small post offices, small-town communities, and one-room country schools seemed to "take the cake" for strange but amusing names. Most people do not know the history of how the places got their names but, perhaps, in most cases it was an incident similar to the one that brought about the name of New Jail School in the eastern part of Douglas County, Missouri. People in this area have told me that the people in this community had build a new school but had not decided on a name. About this time a man was arrested for disturbing the peace. The constable of the township needed to attend a picnic just over the line in another county and did not have time to take the man to jail, all the way to Ava, Missouri, the county seat. So he locked the man in the new schoolhouse over night so he could go to the picnic and do his duty there. The name, New Jail, caught on like fire and everyone seemed pleased with it.

Another version of this name was told to me by Elmer Peterson of Norwood, Missouri. Peterson was a well known educator in southwest Missouri and County Superintendent of Schools of Douglas County, Missouri for many years. He said he heard that when the carpenters finished building the new schoolhouse, they went down to a nearby store and announced that they had finished a new jail for the kids.

People did not lose much sleep worrying about names for places. Perhaps Skunk Hollow was a place inhabited by many skunks; Hog Danger may have been a place where many mean hogs were supposed to be. Black Jack, no doubt, had many trees by this name. Seed Tick probably got it's name as some community minded citizen scratched away at their misery. And they said you could Selmore at Seymour and Seymour at Selmore.

The following is a list of some of the rural schools and the counties in which they were located:

Banner School	Ozark County, Missouri
Oak Mound School	Ozark County, Missouri
Egypt Grove School	Howell County, Missouri
New Jail School	Douglas County, Missouri
	(Later known as Pleasant Mound)
Ball School	Ozark County, Missouri
Louse Level School	Douglas County, Missouri
Possum Trot	Taney County, Missouri
Hog Danger School	Ozark County, Missouri
Black Jack School	Douglas County, Missouri
Huckleberry School	Douglas County, Missouri
Fox School	Stone County, Missouri

Sugar Hill School	Stone County, Missouri
Big Flat School	Baxter County, Arkansas
Needmore School	Ozark County, Missouri
Nubbin Ridge School	Ozark County, Missouri
Buckhorn School	Stone County, Missouri
Flag School	Stone County, Missouri
Barefoot School	Ozark County, Missouri
Chicken Bristle School	Douglas County, Missouri
Lone Star School	Douglas County, Missouri
Mossy Ridge School	Stone County, Arkansas
Pine Log School	Stone County, Arkansas
Endeavor School	Douglas County, Missouri
Beaver School	Douglas County, Missouri
Dogwood School	Douglas County, Missouri
Rock House School	Douglas County, Missouri
Meadow Creek School	Stone County, Arkansas
Seed Tick School	Ozark County, Missouri
Pole Pen School	Douglas County, Missouri
Happy Hollow School	Stone County, Arkansas
West Ridge Woods School	Stone County, Arkansas
East Ridge Woods School	Stone County, Arkansas
Pea Vine School	Douglas County, Missouri
Round Mountain School	Stone County, Arkansas
Leslie School	Searcy County, Arkansas
Allred School	Searcy County, Arkansas

Flat Rock School .... Douglas County, Missouri

Nubbin Ridge School .... Douglas County, Missouri

Cozy Home School .... Searcy County, Arkansas

Victory School .... Douglas County, Missouri

Round Valley School .... Douglas County, Missouri

Welcome Home School .... Searcy County, Arkansas

Highlonesome School .... Douglas County, Missouri

The following is a list of community names, rivers and hollows in the Ozarks. Many of the communities had a post office by the same name.

Old Joe (Community) .... Baxter County, Arkansas

Curall (Community) .... Howell County, Missouri

Sycamore (Community) .... Ozark County, Missouri

Seymour (Town) .... Webster County, Missouri

Hocomo (Community) .... Howell County, Missouri
(Stands for Howell County Missouri)

Longrun (Community) .... Ozark County, Missouri

Birdtown (Community) .... Ozark County, Missouri

Punkin Center (Community) .. Howell County, Missouri

Lily Ridge (Church
    and Cemetery) .... Ozark County, Missouri

Clear Springs (Church
    and Cemetery) .... Ozark County, Missouri

Trail (Community) .... Ozark County, Missouri

Smackout (Community) .... Douglas County, Missouri

Brushy Knob (Community) ... Douglas County, Missouri

Dunn (Community) .... Texas County, Missouri

Bendavis (Community) .... Texas County, Missouri

Ink (Community).....................Shannon County, Missouri

Jerk Tail (Community) .... Wright County, Missouri

Lawndale (Community) .... Ozark County, Missouri

Romance (Community) .... Ozark County, Missouri

Greenbrier (Town).................Faulkner County, Arkansas

Elijah (Community)..................... Ozark County, Missouri

Cedar Gap (Community) .... Wright County, Missouri

Peckerwood Holler (Hollow) .. Douglas County, Missouri

Hunter (River)......................... Douglas County, Missouri

Three Brothers (Community
 and Mountains) .... Baxter County, Arkansas

Lick Creek (River) .... Ozark County, Missouri

Nottinghill (Community).......... Ozark County, Missouri

Turkey Creek (Creek).................. Ozark County, Missouri

Tecumseh (Community)............ Ozark County, Missouri

Sparta (Town).........................Christian County, Missouri

Basher (Community).............. Douglas County, Missouri

Noel (Small Town) ....McDonald County, Missouri

Onion Gap (Road) ....Taney and Douglas
                                                Counties, Missouri

Rome (Community) .... Douglas County, Missouri

Ongo (Community)................. Douglas County, Missouri

Pigeon Creek (Creek)................. Baxter County, Arkansas

Fifty-Six (Community)................Stone County, Arkansas

Sugar Loaf Mountain (Hill) .... Stone County, Arkansas

Lookout Mountain or
   Saul's "Butt" (Hill) .... Douglas County, Missouri

Push Mountain (Hill) .... Baxter County, Arkansas

Devil's Backbone
   (Wilderness Area) .... Ozark County, Missouri

Wild Cherry (Town) .... Fulton County, Arkansas

Rush (Town) .... Marion County, Arkansas

Local Journalism

To be able to write the "items" or the news of a small community for a small town paper in the Ozarks is the delight of many rural farm women and some men who find it interesting. It is a means of releasing tension and a way of getting a free subscription to the paper, which the publisher gives as compensation.

If one checks the "items" of different communities, one will find that there are several common ways of writing such news. It is local and personal. About seventy-five percent or more of the news is about the writer's family. The "items" are about some domestic activity such as doing a big washing, killing hogs, canning corn, or a social event such as a revival meeting, cake suppers, music parties, a marriage, a death or just the simple information that so and so went to visit so and so on Sunday after church last week.

"Items" are just as popular today as they ever were in the Ozarks. All small town papers contain one or more pages of this type of journalism.

Some people make fun of these news items; others ridicule the writer; but most everyone reads them. Editors and publishers realize their popularity and will, no doubt, want to continue with such popular news coverage.

Sometimes this news causes friction in the community. If one woman writes too much about herself or the wrong things, another woman who has been angered may decide to do her own writing about things she considers important. I have know situations like this to arise and the women involved did not speak to one another for months while the contrasting journalism hit the press.

Yet this was and still is a custom in the Ozarks. It is a means of entertainment which reveals much about the people and what they do, what they eat, what they wear, where they go and what they think.

The following lists of "items" will indicate the subjects which are popular:

- Elmer Hunter made hominy last week. He won't let anyone know how he makes it. But it is good. Yours truly ate dinner with them Sunday.
- Miss Sally Hanks was taken to the hospital. She is improving.
- Mr. and Mrs. Joe Smith spent Sunday with Pete Brown.
- Bill Spook has killed a deer.
- A birthday dinner was set for Uncle John Walker last Sunday. This took place at his son's house. Several friends and relatives attended. All had a good time. When they departed, they wished Uncle John many more happy birthdays. He is ninety-eight years old.
- Quite a lot of sore throats around here. Mine is terrible.
- We have had good rains this week.
- John Askew had some carpentry work done last week.
- Seems like everyone is sick around here, including me and the old man.

- My old man got mighty cold runnin' his traps this morning.
- Ed Higgins took a calf to the sale Friday. It sold mighty good.
- Everyone around these parts have enjoyed good messes of squirrel lately.
- Grandma Hope was buried last Saturday. The loved ones have our sympathy.
- Yours truly went with the old man to run his traps one day last week. We had one possum that had crawled into a log. We reached in after him but could only touch the fur. The old man finally had to cut him out.
- Good luck to the newly weds, Joe and Sally. Hope they have a happy life. Sally is my cousin's daughter.
- Yours truly worked on her quilt some last week.
- Anderson Smith has been working for Andy Wilson in the woods. They have been cutting logs for Edley Hiss.
- Mandy Potts stomach has been bothering her lately. She has had the same ailment that yours truly has.
- Sam Levin helped the old man and yours truly haul rocks last evening.
- Fanny Jones will spend the holidays with her son in Arkansas.
- Joseph Stout's fine Jersey cow had a fine set of twin calves last week.
- We sure enjoyed the editoral in last week's paper.
- Candidates have started their smiling again.
- We heard the hounds on the ridge last night.
- Yours truly canned sausage last week.
- Ann Lecker and Joyce Holland drove their kids to school last week cause it was raining.
- Hope Aunt Lula gets well. She is a dear old soul to all of us around here.

- We learned by the grape vine that there is a little lovin' goin' on in the lane past Jack Smith's old barn.
- Church was well attended last night. Brother Loller sure preached a scorcher. Made all of us set up and think. Believe it might have done some good.
- Anyone who has seen a lost dog, please report it to yours truly because she has lost a good black and tan hound. He is a might good old pal. I want him back. He has a light tan color with a white spot on his nose and one on his tail.

Chapter 6

Epitaphs

Among the hills and hollows of the Ozarks the last words have been carved on the stones erected for the dead. How well they represent those for who they have been written, a stranger does not know. But that makes little difference. Yet it seems that one characteristic of Ozark people is to speak well of their dead, no matter what they did in life.

The custom of verses on monuments is no longer as popular as it was in the past. From before the Civil War well into the 20s epitaphs seemed to be a must on many stones. Often they had long verses that seemed to be like a eulogy for the person.

However during the depression years verses became shorter. People did not have the money to be extravagant. Some stones had no epitaph at all.

But in the 40s and 50s epitaphs became popular again but with fewer words. From about the 60s to the present short verses, statements of praise and reverence, a short verse from the Bible, marriage dates and the names of the spouse and children are all that is found. Many stones have no epitaph at all.

It is interesting to note that in many burial places the only stone at the head of the grave is a rock with no inscription at all, not even a name. Yet many family members can locate the grave of one of their own even after fifty or sixty years. However some graves have been lost because the stone has been removed.

The same epitaphs are found in many cemeteries and sometimes on several stones in one cemetery. For example, "Asleep in Jesus," "At Rest," "Called Home," "Gone But Not Forgotten," "Rest in Peace," "Gone Home," "In God We Trust," "We Shall Meet Again," and "At Home With Jesus" are prevalent.

The epitaphs listed in this chapter were found in the following Ozark cemeteries:

Ava Cemetery .... Douglas County, Missouri

Mtn, Grove Cemetery .... Wright County, Missouri

Cabool Cemetery .... Texas County, Missouri

Lone Star Cemetery .... Wright County, Missouri

Denlow Cemetery .... Douglas County, Missouri

Flatwoods Cemetery .... Stone County, Arkansas

Mtn. View Cemetery .... Stone County, Arkansas

Roslawn Cemetery .... Izard County, Arkansas

Galatia Cemetery .... Baxter County, Arkansas

James Cemetery .... Ozark County, Missouri

Lebanon Cemetery .... Laclede County, Missouri

Myetta Cemetery .... Camden County, Missouri

Girdner Cemetery .... Douglas County, Missouri

Seymour Cemetery................. Webster County, Missouri

Maple Park Cemetery .... Greene County, Missouri

Gainesville Cemetery................. Ozark County, Missouri

Blanche Cemetery .... Douglas County, Missouri

West Plains Cemetery .... Howell County, Missouri

Sparta Cemetery .... Christian County, Missouri

Taneyville Cemetery .... Taney County, Missouri

Ozarks Memorial Cemetery-Branson .... Taney County, Missouri

Budded On Earth To Bloom In Heaven

Faith, Hope, Charity

A Tender Mother And a Faithful Friend

We Miss You

Answered The Savior's Call

Thy Memory Shall Be A Guiding Star to Heaven

Resting Until Resurrection Morn

Our Darling Son Is Now Asleep
Jesus Took Him to Keep

Safe In The Hallowed
Quiets Of The Past

A Loving Wife
A Mother Dear
A Faithful Friend
Is Buried Here

A Loved One From Us Has Gone
A Voice We Loved Is Stilled
A Place Is Vacant In Our Hearts
Which Never Can Be Filled

Farewell My Husband and Children
From Your Wife And Mother
Christ Doth Call

Our Little Angel

Absent From The Body
Present With The Lord

Gone To Life And Not To Death
From Darkness To Life's Natural Sky
Come From Sickness And Pain
To Heaven And Immortality

Dear Is The Spot
Where Christ Is Sleep
O Why Should We In Anguish Weep
They Are Not Lost But Gone Before

The Railroad Train
Drove Over The Tracks
Pressing On The Ties
That Jim Has Hacked
Jim Left Miles Of Fence
That Stood Up Yet Held Up
By Post That He Had Split
Jim's Race Finally Came To An End
His Grave Was Dug By Three Of His Friends
When He Died, It Was Quite A Shock
His Friends Went In And Put Him Up This Rock.

God Blesses An Early Death

And Takes The Infant Unto Himself

They Gave Their Today For Our Tomorrow

First Grave In The Cemetery

Together Forever

Resting In Hope Of A
Glorious Resurrection

He Was The Sunshine Of Our Home
He Died As He Lived-A Christian

His Toils Are Past
His Work Is Done
He Fought The Fight-The Victory Won

I Have Fought A Good Fight,
I Have Finished The Course,
I Have Kept The Faith.

You In Our Midst No Longer Stay
To Cheer Me Up With Thy Love
I Hope To Meet With Thee Again
In Your Bright World Above

God Buries His Workmen
But Carries On His Works

Thine Eyes Have Seen The King In His Beauty
Thou Beholdest The Lord That Is Afar Off.

There Are Thoughts That Never Perish
Bright Unfolding Thoughts Of You
So Thy Memory We Cherish
Shined In Hope Embalmed In Tears

Father Let Thy Grace Be Given
That We May Meet In Heaven

In Thee Lord, Have I Put My Trust

Beloved One Thou Are Gone
But Not Forgotten

I Am Gone To Be With My Savior.
Meet Me There.

It Was On Father's Good Pleasure
To Give Us The Kingdom.

Weep Not
They Are At Rest

She Always With A Smiling Face
Would Greet Us At The Door
O How We Miss The Smiles
Since _____ Is No More.

He Is Not Dead But Sleepeth.

Rest Mother, Rest In Quiet Sleep
While Friends In Sorrow
O'er Thee Weep

Weep Not Father And Mother
For I Am Waiting In Glory For Thee.

God Is Greater Than
Any Problem I Have.

Calmly He Sleeps
Beside The One He Dearly Loved

Gone From Our Home
But Not From Our Hearts

A Loving Mother With Strong Convictions
They Were The Sunshine Of Our Home

Remember Friend
While Passing By
Where You Are Now Once Was I
Where I Am Now You Soon Will Be
Prepare For Death And Follow Me.

Gone Home To Live In The House Of The Lord
Dear One We Will Meet Again
Only God Knows When

The Lord Said Unto Me
Lord Sit Thou At My Right-
Hand Until He Make Thine
Enemies My Footstool.

He Was A Poor Man's Friend

A Friend To His Country And
A Believer In Christ.

Tred Softly Stranger
Mother Lies Buried Here

A Story In Jesus, Blessed Thought

Death Is Eternal, Why Should We Weep

Though Thou Art Gone
Fond Memories Cling To Thee

Thy Memory Shall Ever Be
A Guiding Star To Heaven

Kind And Loving
Were Your Ways
Faithful, Fond And True

None Knew Thee But To Love Thee

Blessed Are The Dead
Who In Sorrow Died;
From Our Life's Labor
They Shall Rest On High

Our Love Goes With You
Our Souls Wait To Join You

Farewell Dear Wife And
Children All
A Father Christ
From You Must Call

Weep Not For Me
It Is In Vain
To Call Me To Your
Sight Again

His Book Is Closed
His Life Work Is Done
He Has Gone To A Home
Where Grief Cannot Come

Though We Miss You Much
We Know You Rest With God
The Rose May Fade. The Lily Die.
But The Flowers Immortal Bloom On High.

All Things We Love And Cherish
Like Ourselves Must Fade And Perish

Murdered By One Whom
Name Not Worthy Of Mention (sic)

To Be Lost In The Tunnel Of Life
Now Found By The Light Of Infinity

And Those Who Have Never Know Sorrow
Cannot Know The Infinite Peace
That Falls On The Troubled Spirit
When It Finds At Last Release.

Loving And Kind In All His Ways
Upright And Just To The End Of His Days,
Sincere And True In Heart And Mind
What A Beautiful Memory He Left Behind

May The Resurrection Find You
In The Bosom Of Thy Lord

We Trust Our Loss
Will Be Her Gain
And That With Christ
She's Gone To Reign

Max Decker, Ed. D.

Another Link Is Broken
In Our House Hold (sic)
But A Chain Is Forming
In A Better Land

Warm Summer Sun Shine
Softly Here;
Warm Southern Wind Blow
Softly Here;
Green Sod Above Lie Light

Goodnight, Dear Heart
Goodnight, Goodnight. Lie Light

Chapter 7

Remedies

The information on remedies was told to me by my grandmother, Tennessee James Martin and other people at gatherings, the country store and at any place we decided to talk in southern Missouri and northern Arkansas.

People used remedies for many of their health problems but ladies of the Ozarks had a desire to make themselves look beautiful. My grandmother told me that a piece of damp red cloth was often used for lipstick or rouge. To protect their long beautiful hair, which many women had, plentiful amounts of rainwater was used to wash it. To the rainwater they added egg whites, used coffee and spunk water. To add a feminine smell the ladies used vanilla extract or pulverized blossoms of flowers for perfume.

But most of the remedies were used when people got sick. Frank McClendon of Gainesville, Missouri, told me about having two carbuncles on his foot when he was a boy. Doctors were not able to give him any relief. One day his grandmother saw his condition. She said she would take care of those carbuncles. She asked his mother for a white cloth about three feet long and a foot wide. She went out in the barn lot and got a fresh pile of cow manure that had just passed from the cow, put the hot manure on the cloth and wrapped it around his foot. The next morning she came back and got a milk bottle and filled it with boiling water. She then emptied the bottle and placed the spout of the bottle over each carbuncle. The vacuum in the bottle caused the carbuncles to pop out into the bottle. She saved his foot.

Although most of these remedies in this chapter were used at sometime, it is not the purpose of this author to recommend them.

One of the most interesting remedies was one for stopping bleeding. It had some supernatural qualities as well as being a well-known remedy. Only a few people had the power to be a blood stopper. Yet those who had the power were often called on to do their job. In the community of Dawt, Missouri, Uncle Jack could be depended on to do his best when called. He would come to the bleeding person's house and take a close look at the wound. He would then utter some mysterious words for a few minutes. Some people thought that he was saying a prayer but no one knew for sure. Soon after this he would go to the barn and throw his knife into the ground three times. Next, he would go to a field by himself for some time. The bleeding was supposed to be stopped by the time he got back to his patient. If the bleeding was severe, Uncle Jack used the same method but with much less time involved.

Blood stoppers did not reveal many details about their actions. Uncle Jack said it was a terrible thing for him to die and take these wonderful powers with him. But, if he told his secret to any man, it would never work again. He could tell the secret to another man's wife and she could tell it to another woman and she could tell it to a man and this man would have the power. Or Uncle Jack could have told it to his oldest son and he would have had the power. But Uncle

Jack did not have any boys.

But there were many way of getting medical treatment years ago. Men went to the woods, to the fields, to the rivers and to the mysterious unknown to find a cure.

The following is a list of remedies for some of the more common ailments or diseases:

- If you ever stepped on a rusty nail, soak your foot in coal oil or wrap the nail in a piece of fat meat and throw it on the roof of your house. The wound would heal within three days. And some believed that putting the fat meat on the cut would make it heal and draw out the poison.
- If a baby had trouble with its gums hurting, some people would tie a mole's foot around the baby's neck.
- It was good to drink warm cow's milk for a bad cold.
- Drink nine drinks of water to stop the hiccups.
- Another way to stop the hiccups was to scare the person who has them.
- One more way to stop the hiccups was to pick up a rock, spit in the hole the rock left in the ground and put the rock back in the same place.
- Put flour on a cut to stop bleeding
- To take off warts some people rubbed the wart with a grain of corn and fed the corn to a chicken. Some thought it worked better if you fed it to a black chicken.

One woman in the Bakersfield and Elijah, Missouri area had the power to remove warts. One could call her on the telephone and tell her the location of the wart and she would say thank you and hang up. In a few days the wart would be gone. Or one could go to her house, it was said, and she would touch the wart and it would be gone in a short time.

Other neighborhoods had different ways to get rid of

warts. The person would count the number of warts they had, get a piece of string and tie a knot in it for every wart and hide the string.

Or another good way to get rid of warts was to have someone spit tobacco juice on the wart and let it run off on the ground. Then they would make an X with a stick through the juice. Then they had the person's brother or sister hide the stick. If they could not find the stick, the warts would leave.

A good health booster in the spring was a mess of wild "greens." A good mess would consist of polk, dock, both wide dock, and "nar" narrow dock, wild lettuce, sheep sorrels and dandelions. This was a good mild laxative that people needed in the spring because they had not had much if any leafy vegetables during the winter.

- To add iron to your system, people soaked a rusty nail and drank the water.
- When a baby had the colic, they would blow a puff of smoke up its gown.
- If someone wanted to wean a baby, they started the process when the sign was in the feet.
- Children were always getting something in their eye. To get it out people poured a spoonful of warm milk in it.
- Walnut hull juice placed on the skin will cure poison ivy.
- 'Parsimmon" bark boiled and put in the ear will cure the earache.
- For sick stomach, we ate burned bread.
- People cured snakebite by spreading apple vinegar and salt over the bite.

Anything that grew in the soil seemed to be good for us, or a least that was what our parents and grandparents thought. Pearly Everlasting was called Life Everlasting because nothing ever seemed to bother it. Cattle or horses wouldn't eat it. But it was used by young boys and some girls as tobacco or, at least, it was something that could be rolled and smoked or chewed. It had a strong bitter taste but we chewed it anyway. It acted as a mild laxative if we swallowed the juice.

- For toothache people put splinters of cedar between the teeth.
- Mule tail weed was boiled and used for a sick stomach.
- Heartburn was treated by taking one teaspoon of soda and one-half glass of water.
- Eating raw eggs was good for several things: for a weak stomach, for the colic or to make a child grow faster.
- People treated an old sore that would not heal with a poultice made from molasses and flour.

May Apples or Mandrakes were well known to people of the hills. Although they knew that the roots were poisonous, except when given by a doctor as medicine, they could eat the apple. Many thought that it gave them sexual stimulation and promoted conception.

- Smart weed boiled down was good for fever.
- Putting an ax under the bed was good for pain.

Many children got stone bruises on their feet from running over the rocks and dirt barefooted. They doctored it by putting their feet in warm, fresh cow manure.

Babies often had a sore mouth so the parents had a relative wash the inside of their shoe and took the water and had the baby drink it.

People were always getting a sore throat. To cure it they took off their left shoe and spit in it three times and then rubbed this on their neck.

- Salt is good for a sore throat.
- Another treatment for the stone bruise was a poultice of sweet milk and biscuits.
- People cured a chest cold by mixing lard, kerosene and pepper and rubbing it over the chest.
- To help the whooping cough, one would drink the juice from turnips that had been coated with sugar.
- A sure way to get rid of warts was to pick three drops of blood from the wart and put it in an envelope and drop the envelope at a crossroads. The first person to find it would get your warts.

People in this mountain area were often cut and bleeding in some way, stung by a wasp, exposed to some disease, or had a bad infection. But they had a remedy for these problems.

- Put soot on a cut to stop the bleeding.
- Use a potato or fat meat to draw out infection.
- To cure thrash or thrush in babies, have someone who has never seen the baby's father blow in the mouth of the baby.
- Turpentine and lard mixed together and heated is good for a chest cold if placed in a poultice and applied to the chest.
- To make a cut heal, mix black pepper and sugar and place it on the cut.
- If someone is exposed to the whooping cough, have them go to a creek, catch a small minnow and swallow it. They will not have this disease.
- Make a paste with soda and water for a wasp sting.
- A drop of the juice from a turnip placed in the eye will wash out anything in the eye.
- A tea made from various juices and tea by heating it to almost a boil is good for colds during the winter. People call it Russian tea.

- Put ashes in a bag with hot water and place it on the chest for a chest cold.
- Grease the bottom of your feet and get them hot and you will not have a bad cold.
- Rich cream is good for a sunburn.
- Take the wax out of your ear and put it on your lip or nose to cure a cold sore.
- Honey is good for a sore throat.
- Chewed tobacco or snuff is good for wasp sting.
- Sheep droppings boiled in water will help break out the measles.
- When a dog chases its tail, throw cold water on its head.
- Tie an old dirty sock with garlic in it around your neck for a cold.
- When a cow loses her cud, give her an old dirty dish rag.
- Vinegar and hot water will kill weeds.
- Peach tree leaves boiled down make a good poultice for colds.
- If you stump your toe soak it in coal oil.
- Blackberry wine is good for stomach problems.
- Put a knife under your bed to cut labor pains.
- Sweet cream is good to rub on hives.
- For a cold that won't go away, drink a tablespoon of "moonshine" whiskey three times a day and at bedtime.
- If you get your feet wet during cold weather, come home as soon as possible and soak your wet feet in Epsom salts for two or three hours. By doing this you are preventing a bad cold from starting.
- Get rid of ringworm by rubbing green walnut juice over the ring.

- For colic, take a loaf of bread hot from the oven and cut it in half. Place one half on the abdomen and the other half on your back opposite it.
- To remove a particle of steel from the eye, put a piece of horse's hair over the object, shut the eye and pull the hair out. The steel particle will come out with it.
- To remove something from a child's eye, pour a spoonful of warm milk in it.
- To add iron to your system, eat black haws.
- If your side aches while walking, stop where you are in the road and pick up a rock and spit under it. Place the rock back in the same place and go on down the road without looking back.
- When someone has cold sores or fever blisters as they are sometimes called, drink a glass of buttermilk four times a day and they will disappear in about two days.
- For burns, use vanilla, baking soda, butter, lard, or mustard.
- To remove a sty, go to a crossroad, stand there and say, "Sty, sty, come off my eye and go to the next eye."
- Tea made from boiling punkin seeds will get rid of worms.
- The bark off the north side of a sycamore tree will ease the discomfort of measles if boiled and placed on the skin.
- For hiccups, breathe into a paper bag.
- Tea made from boiling blackberry roots is good for a cold.
- Skunk oil is good for a cold if applied to the chest when the cold first begins.
- Senna tea made by boiling the leaves of the senna plant is a good laxative. Many parents used this tea in the spring time to help their children get rid of worms.

- Boneset tea is good for fever and was a good painkiller.

One can see by these remedies that the hill people of the Ozarks were concerned with warts, hiccups, colds, hives, thrush, rheumatism, earache, shingles, diphtheria, cuts, bleeding, fevers, infections, especially those caused by stepping on a rusty nail, stone bruises, cutting teeth, toothache, rash caused by poison ivy, sties, burns or something in the eye.

Sinus problems were dreaded by hill people. Almost everyone had this problem. One sure cure, many people thought, was to mix salt, sugar and soda with warm water and sniff it up the nose.

Although it was not a remedy, it may have been a prevention in many cases. A woman who was born near the Red Bank, Missouri community told me that she was told that people used Vaseline as a birth control method in the 20s and 30s.

In the 1930s my wife's father became very ill. He had the measles but could not get them to "break out." One of their neighbors was the son of a freed slave and visited them often. He recommended to the family that they make a tea from sheep droppings and have him drink the tea three times a day.

Some communities in the Ozarks were fortunate enough to have someone with the power to blow the fire out of a burn. This person had to believe their power would work. It could be passed down from a female to a male and by a male on to a female in that order. Usually the person who could do this quoted some passage from the Bible. In a very short time the burn would no longer hurt. This person was in great demand because someone was often burning themselves on the stove as they put wood in it.

Although many people used these remedies, including this writer, it is not the purpose of this account of remedies to recommend them to this generation.

Chapter 8

Times for Planting

The information I have collected about times for planting came from my mother, Gladys Martin Decker, and my grandmother, Tennessee James Martin and from various neighbors in south central Missouri and northern Arkansas. Each year during late winter and spring months there was much talk about when to plant crops and when to make garden. All one had to do was just listen.

Rural farmers and many small town people in the Ozarks were concerned as much about the time for planting as they were about being careful on Friday 13. However, a large majority will tell you that signs did not work in all cases but they still believe in them with all their heart. The light and dark of the moon seems to be the center of this belief that must be observed if a good crop of anything is desired.

Of course modern agricultural scientists at the state and university level and local agricultural agents scoff at these practices. However, no one will dispute the fact that just about any farmer who watches the signs and times of the moon has a green thumb and can grow more in one hill than a poor university trained, high salaried county agent can grow on an acre.

In addition to times for planting and harvesting, there are times for marking cattle and hogs. Anyone in the

Ozarks knows that if you want an animal to die by bleeding to death, just mark it when the sign is in the heart.

It is old Mother Nature that rules the seasons, they believe. It is she that shifts the moon and the stars. It is she that arranges the signs which must be used in any relationship with her.

There are signs in the Ozarks for planting just about anything. The following are a few of the signs widely used in the Ozarks for planting:

- Good Friday is the time to plant potatoes.
- When the leaves of a hickory tree get the size of a squirrel's ear, it is time to plant corn.
- Plant cucumbers on the one-hundredth day of the year.
- Oats--When you want grain, plant in the dark of the moon. When you want straw, plant in the light of the moon.
- Plant pine trees when the snow is on the ground and no air will get to the roots. They will grow well.
- When whippoorwills first sing in the spring, it is time to plant peas.
- In July, if the sign is in the neck on the first or second day, one should plant radishes, potatoes and onions.
- Plant late corn after the sixth day of June.
- Plant cabbage and tomatoes when the sign is in the head.
- Beans and cucumbers should be planted under the sign of the twins.
- When Pee Wee's[6] time for singing comes in the spring, it is time to plant corn.
- Plant anything that grows underground in the dark of the moon.
- Plant anything that grows on top of the ground in the light of the moon.

- Go out before sun up, do not speak to anyone, and wear your old split bonnet. If you plant your sweet potatoes under such conditions, they will produce well.
- Plant potatoes as early as possible on the first pretty day in February.

People took care to know the signs because they not only planted a large garden but many had a "truck-patch" which was a large garden maybe as much as an acre or two. Sometimes they sold some of the vegetables they grew. Many times they gave them to their neighbors and they canned as much as they could for the next winter's food. Garden making was serious business in the Ozarks and still is. However, not as many people "make garden" as they did fifty or sixty years ago.

Farmers in the Ozarks liked to find a calendar that had Zodiac signs.[7]

Since one of the major ways of making a living in the Ozarks was farming, people had to have a stout team of horses to pull a Number 10 Oliver or larger plow to "turn the soil" to make a good seedbed. There were other brands of turning plows that were sold but in many sections of the Ozarks the farmer liked the Oliver the best. They had to have some type of "horse-drawn" plow since most of them did not have tractors.

They needed a small horse or mule with small feet to plow a garden or "truck patch" or a field of corn. Large horses that were used to pull a "turning plow" would not work well pulling a "double shovel." They would step on too many plants with their big feet.

Farmers trained their horses and mules how to turn and when to turn. A good horse or mule or a team of either would soon learn to turn to the right if the farmer said "gee" and turn to the left if they said "haw." "Get-up" meant for the team or horse or mule to start forward. "Back-up" meant for the animals to move back.

A good farmer in the Ozarks had to have different types of machinery to grow corn or to make a garden or "truck patch." Of course the "turning plow" was used first. After the soil was turned they leveled it with a harrow (har). A spring-tooth harrow was probably the best to work the soil but it pulled up too many rocks. So many farmers made themselves a harrow called an "A" harrow because it was in the shape of an A. It did not pull up as many rocks. It had heavy steel spikes that were driven through holes that were drilled in the timbers.

At the end was a double-tree to which the single-trees for each horse was attached. The single-trees supported the traces on the horse which connected the harness on the horse to the harrow.

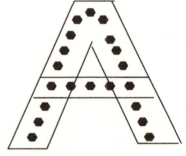

An "A" harrow or "har"

Often, if the harrow needed more weight, the farmer would stand on the cross-timber holding the reins and guide the horses. Or sometimes they would place a large rock on the harrow for more weight.

Next they used a "drag" to break up clods of dirt and level the soil even more. A "drag" was made by tying two chains to a log about eight feet long and about six inches in diameter. The chains were attached to a double-tree so the team of horses could pull it. The farmer stood on the "drag" and held the reins to the team. Sometimes when they went over a large rock, the farmer was forced to step off or be thrown off.

An important field crop in the Ozarks was corn. People needed corn for animal feed and corn to take to the nearest mill to be ground into meal to make cornbread and mush.

Most farmers planted their corn, two grains to a hill, with a "Blue-Jay" corn planter that they pushed into the soil as they pulled a lever at the top to release the corn. But there were a few farmers who could afford a "horse drawn" planter.

But what machine to use if the farmer was lucky enough to have both made a big difference. The one that would get the corn into the soil the correct depth, not too shallow, not too deep, was the one that they must use. The way the corn was planted determined how much corn they would grow that season.

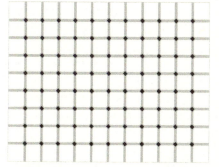

The farmer "checked" his cornfield by making rows north and south and east and west. This made the corn easier to plow with the "double-shovel" and they were able to keep the weeds from growing too much near his corn plants. After he had plowed the corn several times or until it was too tall to put a horse between the rows, he considered it "laid-by" and did not need anymore plowing that season.

The farmer watched his children carefully or whoever was planting the corn to see that they planted at the

A Double Shovel

same point on the check each time. If they were off an inch or two, it made plowing more difficult and the rows did not look good to neighbors who might pass by his field.

A Turning Plow, Left A Double Shovel, Right

So the farmer in the Ozarks did the following things to grow a "patch" of corn, a garden or a "truck-patch": They plowed the soil with a "turning plow." Then they ran a harrow (har) over the soil to break the clods of dirt. Then if the soil was not level enough for them they used a drag.

A Layin-Off Plow

Next they "laid-off" the rows with a "layin-off" plow and then planted the corn or other seeds with a hand planter or "horse drawn" planter. Sometimes they just used a hoe. One person went along the row and dug a small hole in the ground. The next person came along and dropped two grains of corn in the hole. Then a third person came along and covered the corn or whatever it was with soil. This person usually used a lighter weight hoe so they would not get too much soil over the seeds. To do this job by using only hoes, it was an advantage if the farmer had a large family.

Dropping the corn and covering it with a hoe or using a hand planter was a hard job on a hot spring day. A story was told that one farmer sent three of his boys out to the field one day to plant the corn with hand planters. After a time the farmer went out in his field to see how much of his corn had come up. Or, as most people in the Ozarks would say, what kind of stand he had got. But to his amazement about one-half of the field had no young plants at all. As he wondered about this and looked around, he found about two or three gallon of corn in a stump near the field. Everyone in the community knew what had happened and was rather sure what happened to the boys when their father got them "out behind the barn."

A "Horse Drawn" Corn Planter

Farmers in this region of the country not only wanted a good team of horses or mules but also a good set of harness. The following picture is of a young man and his wife ready to go to the field for a long day of work. This picture was taken in 1920 in Ozark County, Missouri near the community of Tecumseh.

In addition to wanting a good team of horses or mules and good equipment, farmers in the Ozarks were particular about where they planted their garden or "truck patch."

They liked to grow many of their crops in "new ground." "New Ground" was soil that had not been used for years. It was usually covered with sprouts, stumps of old trees, weeds and rocks. It was difficult to plow and hard to make a seedbed but it was rich soil and would grow about anything. People liked to grow green beans, corn for canning and pumpkins in it, as well as other vegetables.

It seemed just right to grow pumpkins. About everyone liked "punkin pie." Often at pie suppers the "guess pie" would be called New Ground Punkin.

It was a familiar sight in early summer time, especially, to see my father and neighbors far down in the field plowing corn. I could hear them saying "gee, haw, back, get up and whoa." When they would get to the end of the field, I could hardly see them move. Their sounds were interrupted by crows in the morning and afternoon and crickets, katydids and tree frogs about the time the sun went down. But I could still hear them talking to their horses or mules. When they said "Whoa" I knew they were ready for a drink of water kept cold by a gunny sack soaked in cold water and wrapped around a half gallon fruit jar of water. It stayed cold enough to drink for about an hour.

Then I had to run to the house, draw cold water from the well and fill another jar and bring it back to the end of the field where he would take a big drink and turn the horse or mule around and start on another row.

Chapter 9

Signs of the Weather

People have always put much faith in signs they used to predict the weather. To have lived in the first part of this century gives one much knowledge about these signs. People believed that certain things indicated a change in the weather and they prepared for it. My grandmother, Tennessee James Martin, knew the signs listed here and dozens more.

When the moon is in a position so that a powder horn can be hung on it, there will be rain. When this cannot be done, it will be dry and no rain will come for some time.

When corn husks are thick, look out for bad weather the following winter.

Rainbow at night, sailor's delight. Rainbow at morning, sailor's warning.

If you kill a snake, take it by the tail and throw it over your shoulder. If it lands with its stomach upward to the sky, there will be rain within the next twenty-four hours. If it lands with its back toward the sky, there will be no rain for many days.

These are only a few of the many signs that make United States Weather Bureau people blush, but they are signs that helped many people get their hay in the barn without getting it wet or allowed them to go fishing when the fish were biting.

Most people who forecast the weather by signs believe that weather conditions are caused by phases and location of the moon.

The following signs have been divided into these categories: rain, bad weather, good weather, snow-cold, good and bad weather, a change in the weather and frost.

Rain
- If the wind blows and you can see the under side of a silver maple leaf, a rainstorm is coming.
- Rain before seven, quit before eleven.
- When you hear turtle doves singing, it will rain soon.
- When the sun shines while it is raining, it will rain the same time the next day.
- Three frosts in a row will be followed by the rain.
- If a cat eats grass, it will rain soon.
- When you hear tree frogs, it is a sign of rain.
- If it rains on Monday, it will rain three days that week.
- If water hangs in drops on a wire fence, there will be rain.
- When rocks sweat, there will be rain soon.
- If the sun sets behind a cloud on Wednesday, it will rain before Sunday.
- If the wind blows for three days from the south, it will rain.
- If leaves on trees curl, there will be rain.
- If a rabbit barks, it is a sign of rain.
- If the sun has streaks below it, it is a sign of rain.
- The sun drawing water is a sign of rain.
- When fish swim near the surface of the water, there will be rain soon.
- If chickens rest in the sun, it will rain.
- When it is raining and chickens fly on a fence and pick themselves, the rain is going to stop. If they do not do this, it will rain all day.

- A southwest wind will bring rain.
- If lightning bugs fly close to the ground, it will rain soon.
- A cricket chirping loudly is a sign of rain.
- If you see a whirlwind, it will rain within three days.
- When a rooster crows after sunset, it will rain soon.
- When animals turn their back to the wind, it is going to rain.
- When dogs want to stay on the porch, rain will come soon.

Bad Weather

- If lady bugs swarm in the fall, look out for a spell of weather early in winter.
- If you hear an owl hoot in the daytime, a storm is coming.
- If the sky becomes cloudy when a frost is on the ground, there will be bad weather.
- The higher turkeys roost in a tree, the colder the winter will be.
- If cows are restless and bunch together, there will be stormy weather.
- If your nose itches, bad weather will come.
- When your bones seem to ache, the weather will get bad.
- When smoke goes to the ground, there will be bad weather.
- If a cat licks its paws, there will be stormy weather.
- When much moss grows on the north side of a tree, the weather will be bad.
- If cows bawl for no reason, there will be bad weather.
- If it thunders in January, there will be much more bad weather.
- If a chicken crows after it has flown up to roost, bad weather is on the way.

- If there is a full moon with a circle around it, there will be bad weather in a few days.
- If an animal grows a thick coat of hair, there will be a cold winter.
- When turtles begin to crawl, it is a sign of bad weather.
- If you go hunting and find no game, the weather will get bad.
- The number of circles around the moon tells the number of days before bad weather.
- Fluffy white clouds are a sign of dry weather.
- When birds fly high in the sky, terrible heat will come.
- When it is very still and you can hear noise far away, there will be bad weather coming.

Good Weather
- If the sun sets clear, the next day will be pretty.
- A cotton sky indicates a clear day tomorrow.

Snow and Cold
- A flight of snowbirds feeding is a sign of snow.
- When fire pops in the stove or fireplace, there will be snow.
- If snow stays on the ground very long, it is waiting for another snow.

Good and Bad Weather

The shape of the growth inside a persimmon seed will predict a good or bad winter as follows:
- Shaped like a spoon: Plenty of snow that winter.
- Shaped like a fork: Not much snow that winter.
- Shaped like a knife: Cutting cold that winter.

A Woolly Worm that is seen in the fall will indicate by its color whether the winter will be good or bad as follows:

- Dark color all over--Bad winter
- Light color all over--Mild winter
- Dark on one end near its head--Bad winter early
- Light color in the middle--Mild winter in mid-winter
- Dark color near tail--Bad winter late.

A Change in the Weather
- When horses run and play in the field, there will be bad weather.
- Blue sky in the morning, sailors take warning.
- If you see a sun dog in the sky, there will be a change in the weather. (Sun dogs are bright spots near the sun.)
- If calves run and play in the barnyard, there will be a change in the weather.
- When ducks or geese fly south, it is a sign that winter is near. When they fly north, spring is just around the corner.
- When you see many birds flying, there will be a change in the weather.

Frost
- Thunder in February means frost in May.
- If you hear locusts sing in September, count six weeks ahead and that day will bring the first killing frost.
- It will be three months from the time the first katydid sings until frost.

Miscellaneous
- If hornets build their nest close to the ground, it will be a light winter.
- One extreme weather condition calls for another. For example, if it is warm in November and December, there will be bitter cold in a few weeks.

Chapter 10

Entertainment

People have entertained themselves well from the time of the early settlements. During the nineteenth century the quilting bee, the house raising, the log rollings and the dance and music were enjoyable means of fun. This continued into the frontier period, during World War I, during the Great Depression, through World War II and into the 1950s. Perhaps the reason for the great enjoyment of doing the things mentioned above was the fact that much of the fun was associated with some type of work that the people needed to get done.

Entertainment was good for the men and women. They worked hard all during the week. And while at work their minds turned to what they were going to do that night or that weekend. This moved them on in their work as it gave them something to look forward to.

From the 1920s to World War II is, perhaps, the most interesting period to notice. For during this time the Depression and the environment just before the war helped to create types of entertainment quite unlike that of any other day. Many of these same activities are practiced today but faster means of communication take people further away from the community center, the one-room schoolhouse. There still are a few schoolhouses of this type, but for the most part they no longer exist.

These people had a variety of ways to entertain themselves. They enjoyed having pie suppers, community picnics, cake suppers at their neighbor's house, and play parties for the younger ones. They enjoyed songs, singing and about any type of country music. They read about anything they could get their hands on. They loved playing tricks on each other. There was a trickster in every community. They told jokes and short stories, enjoyed talking over the telephone and listening to others talk and anytime they had a chance, they, or at least most of them, liked to dance. They made a big "to do" about weddings and charivaris, taking pictures and filling in the time on slow weekends with a case of Kangaroo Court. They had fun shooting anvils, cotton rocks and shot guns on holidays and they paid their respects to their loved ones and neighbors who had died when they gathered at the cemetery or "grave yard" on Memorial Day or "Decoration Day!"

The Pie Supper

A pie supper was one of the most enjoyed events. They were held for many reasons in addition to having fun. There was the Red Cross, The March of Dimes, the USO or the need to raise money to roof the schoolhouse or to reinforce the ladies' outhouse which had been bombarded by the boys on Halloween. Yet the major purpose was for something to do, to have some fun and to get together with the neighbors.

Families always started doing the chores early on the night of the pie supper. Mothers rubbed the necks and ears of their children to a red clean to accompany the haircut they had given them that afternoon. The boys were decked out in clean overalls. The girls had on their best dresses, starched as stiff as a board.

Our family always went early because Mom wanted to get a seat by the stove and Dad wanted to chew the fat with the boys before the event began.

The men and boys stood around outside and watched the women bring the bright colored boxes with strips of crepe paper and ribbon flying.

Young men and boys liked to stay on the outside and peek in through the windows or play tag in the dark or hang around and listen to the older men talk. However, at times the men seemed to want the boys to leave them alone near the fence that ran down by the schoolhouse. So they sent the smaller ones scampering into the darkness for another game of tag.

The men seemed to like to go down under the hill from the schoolhouse to the open-air toilet and talk and talk. They usually came back in better spirits for they would be laughing and talking as loud as they could about something that boy of mine did, or something else that interested them.

"Whar's that boy of mine? Let me tell you, that kid, that damn kid of mine, to me, is the smartest kid around here." Or it might be a conversation about a "grass widow" in the community. "Sadie King's comb is sure red since her old man died. And he's only been gone about three weeks. Might be we aughta watch her around for a spell."

This talking, accompanied by smoking and chewing, went on for some time. But it wasn't long until Si Watts, who always did the selling of the pies, came to the door and began to call the folks together.

"Hey! Hey! Hey! Could I get your attention? We are about ready to begin this here pie supper. Young men, get

2 Soon 2 Be 4 Gotten

in a good position so you can see your gal's pie. Quiet please. Quiet."

This took some time because the men had not seen the women in several minutes and were in a good mood to do some talkin'.

Si Watts was an enjoyable character. He was big with rosebud cheeks and a round head. He had a big belly that made his blue overalls too tight if he buttoned them on the sides. So he just forgot about that. He would never have harmed a flea but he could auctioneer in his own way which was not worth a darn. Yet folks got a big kick out of listening to him and watching him. He was the pride of the supper, the master of the schoolhouse, the man who sold the pies.

His introduction usually went something like this: "Ladies and Gentlemen, as we have congregated ourselves here to show good faith to one another and enjoy this here night and try our darndest to raise money enough to build the ladies a fittin' place to go when they need to _____."

From this, everything got underway. Pies were sold first to the highest bidder. In the 1930s they sold from 15¢ to $1 depending on the neatness and color of the box and whose pie it was. Now and then some man would run a pie up on some young boy who showed by his actions that he would buy that pie or die trying. Sometimes in this case the pie might bring as much as $3 or $4 or more.

The guess pie came next. Some lady baked a pie and donated it to the supper. Anyone could guess what kind it was for 1¢ a guess. The person who made the correct guess got the pie. It usually turned out to be persimmon butter, new-ground punkin or up-side-down pie or something like that.

Next came a nice new pair of cotton work socks for the

man with the dirtiest feet. One could vote for someone by going to the front of the schoolhouse and paying 5¢ for each vote. The man, never a woman in those days, who had the dirtiest feet had to come to the front, wash his feet in a wash tub and put on his new socks. In the 30s not very many people complained about getting a new pair of socks.

Every pie supper had a rooster to give to the man voted as the most hen-pecked husband. Sometimes this made the wife a little angry and she eyed the people who were voting for her husband. But the crowd laughed and clapped their hands and laughed some more.

Someone got a sack of tobacco for the biggest tobacco bum. This may have hurt the winner a little but he was glad to get the tobacco anyway.

A jar of pickles was given to the most lovesick couple. After the selection was made at 5¢ a vote, the dreamy eyed kids came from the back corner after much kidding and accepted the prize.

The most moneymaking venture was the box of candy for the prettiest girl. Often two boys would be running their girls for the honor and would give every cent they had to try to win the prize.

After all the different events were completed, the auctioneer announced how much money had been made and that it was now time for anyone who had bought a pie to find the person who had baked it. This took several minutes, but it wasn't long until boys were bashfully gulping down the pie that they had paid their last cent for and men were kidding other men about eating with their wives. At midnight everyone was about ready to go home but they would never forget the pie supper. It was always discussed over the neighborhood for several months as old men, boys and women looked forward to the next pie supper for the purpose of raising money for a worthy cause.

But everything wasn't happy and cheerful at some pie suppers. Often anywhere in the Ozarks someone could stop all the good clean fun in just a few minutes. Sometimes it seemed that some people just came to the pie supper to cause trouble. Knucks, knives, whiskey and women caused trouble now and then.

Wayne Powell who lives in Ava, Missouri now lived in Eminence for a good part of his teen-age years. One time Wayne and a friend went to a pie supper in that part of the Ozarks. They took two girls from the community. One of the girls had been "sparkin" another boy who, with a friend, were at the pie supper drunk.

Wayne's friend asked him to buy one girl's pie so the boy wouldn't get mad at him. So he bought the pie and handed it to his friend as soon as he bought it.

Well, this made the other boy mad and he began to fight Wayne's friend, hitting him with knucks. He also grabbed the distributor cap out of Wayne's car, threw it high in the air and shot at it with a pistol.

The boy with the brass knucks almost killed the other boy. The older people in the schoolhouse came out and stopped the fight and began to look for Wayne's distributor cap. They looked and looked and finally found it not too far away.

On the way home Wayne said he stopped at a crossing on Jack's Fork and washed the blood off his truck.

Picnics

My parents, E.C. and Gladys Decker, my uncles, friends at the country store and my own experiences gave me the information about picnics in the Ozark Mountains. Counties such as Douglas and Ozark in southern Missouri would have four or five picnics over the county in one summer.

People came from everywhere to the picnic. They were there from Needmore, Seed Tick, Hog Danger, Sand Ridge, Champion, Cross Roads, and everywhere else.

One of the best like attractions was the carnival. The glimmer of the lights on the large wheel that went around and around was like "forty-leven" big lanterns floating in the sky.

There were some people there that they called gypsies. They had all their clatter and fortune telling and now and then there would be some lady fortune-teller who, as people say, was not exactly on the "up and up." A man from near Tecumseh, Missouri, told me about an incident that happened at the Steel Bridge Picnic at Tecumseh. He said that one of them fortune-tellers got one of the old men of the community into her tent, but when he came out his pocket book was gone and fifty dollars with it. When he found he had lost his money, he started yelling that that pretty little snake had stolen his money and he was lookin' for the sheriff to help him. The money was recovered but old Jack never did stop talking about that pretty little gal in that tent that thought she had got into his mind and thought she would fool him into letting her steal his money.

There was always fiddle music and a dance floor. The owner of the floor usually started his campaign for dancers at about five o'clock in the afternoon. "Ten at the gate, ten at the door, ten to see these pretty gals hop out on the floor." Not only the dancers had to pay but the owner would accept money from anyone who just wanted to stand and watch. They two-stepped, waltzed, jigged and square danced.

When a square dance was going someone might be on

the corner jigging. One man liked to dance so much that he danced with a broom when he could not find a partner.

The dancing continued until after midnight. There was a large crowd around the floor at all times. The hot weather did not seem to affect the dancers and those who like it. The dancers just wiped sweat and kept on mauling the floor and swinging their partners. The caller stood on the corner of the floor and clapped his or her hands and now and then knocked out a little jig by themselves to add to the show. One of the calls that everyone seemed to enjoy went something like this:

Chicken in the bread pan pickin' out dough.
Granny will your dog bite? No, chile, no.
Circle eight and promenade.
Swing that lady.
Don't be afraid.
Everybody swing . . .
Three little sisters standin' in a row.
Swing the one that wants to go.
Promenade.
Keep em off the corner.
Swing your partner.
Circle up eight.
Allemande left.

There was always some moonshine to be found at the picnic. If it wasn't colored with brown sugar or something it looked just like water. But one drink of that water and you were drunk. Some people just drank too much of it and passed out. I remember going to a picnic in a southern Missouri county one evening and looking along the path to the picnic grounds at young men and old men stretched out in the shade of a tree or in the sun, unconscious.

Somebody always had a fight at the picnic. The event wasn't much fun unless during the three days it lasted there was four or five fights. It seems that if a man or a family had trouble during the year with another man or family that they saved it until the picnic to be settled. And they settled it with whatever they could find to use. They used rocks, tire tools, clubs, brass knucks and if nothing else could be found, their fists. They often used knives, also. They cut each other, bled, cursed and seemed to try to kill each other. When one man went down, the other piled on top of him and beat at his face with his fists or something until he said he had had enough. Wives cried, children screamed and neighbors got mad. Soon another fight might break out.

Men seemed not to be afraid of anything or anyone. In fact, they seemed to enjoy the fighting. And the moonshine gave them courage to fight and fight and fight. "A little bit of that stuff won't hurt anyone," they said.

One time at the Dora picnic in Ozark County, Missouri a family had been feuding all year over something that they didn't talk about. They had been thinking about it all year and there seemed to be no better place to settle it than at the picnic. So they started yelling at each other and calling each other names so soon someone hit one of the others and the fight was on. They would let two fight while the others looked on yelling encouragement at their man.

As two of the men were fighting, a small man who acted like a "banty" rooster most of the time, ran out from the circle of people that surrounded the fight. He was not taking sides, just wanting some attention. Immediately after he stepped out a little too far, someone who thought he might be against them threw a rock that hit him just above the left ear. He fell like a stuck hog. Several from the crowd dragged him to a shade tree, left him there to come-to and the fight went on.

Later on that evening a man started to climb into an old flat bed truck to beat up on the man on the truck. The man on the truck said, "I've got my family here on the truck with me and I don't want any trouble with you. I ain't ever bothered you. I got my wife, my mother and five little girls here with me and I don't want any trouble." But the man on the ground cursed, yelled and called him names and made a move like he was going to climb on the truck after the man. He put his hands on a board which was part of the shallow bed of the truck like he was going to climb in. When he put his hands on the truck bed, the man in the truck hit his hands with a tire tool. His hands were broken, crushed. Blood spurted from the wound. He yelled in pain, holding one crushed hand with the other as blood ran all over him and the ground. Someone soon came after him and took him away as he continued to scream with pain. Soon the man on the truck took his family and left for home and the crowd broke up and started to look for something else exciting.

The hamburger stand was a gathering place for everyone. It seemed that a burger was just a little better down there at the picnic. The operators of these stands were not from a state health department. One big fellow as long as anyone can remember was the "hamburgerest maker" anyone ever saw. He rolled those little balls of meat and patted them so firmly that they looked like little balls of mud. And nobody ever cared if he washed his hands or not. They just ate all the ten cent burgers they could hold, drenched them down with a cold glass of lemonade, then headed back toward the dance floor. No amount of dirt, sand, filthy grease from the man's hands could seem to harm the taste of the bread-filled meat balls made by the man who ran the stand.

Sometimes during the three-day affair the politicians, if it happened to be an election year, were given a chance to express their views and solicit the vote of those who were present. The most popular candidate was the one who promised everybody something and after his speech announced that if anyone would go to the stand, there would be hamburgers and drinks for all voters and their children.

Sometimes candidates for state and national offices came. It was not uncommon for candidates for United States Representative to be there. The chairperson of the Republican and Democrat parties would introduce them sometime during the day when the most people were there and they would get on a stump or a little platform and say a few words, words good enough to get some votes.

One candidate that everyone in southwest Missouri just about remembers was a great orator. One time he was making a speech about a statement his opponent had made.

"My opponent brags about his experiences and his travels over the country and the world. Well don't let that fool you, my good friends. I have been further back under the barn after eggs than he has been away from home."

Everyone laughed. They liked that. He seemed to be a common man. Maybe he had been under the barn after eggs sometime. We'll just vote for a man like that. And they did. He was elected to office twelve or thirteen terms.

After all the picnics were over, neighbors talked about them all year. And if they had any problems with their neighbors, they let it simmer for a year until the next picnic and then many of them fought over it.

Cake Suppers

The cake supper was a frequent type of entertainment in the Ozark Mountains. At least once a month someone in the neighborhood who had a girl or girls who wanted to catch a feller would have a supper. Everyone was invited and everyone came. Each family was asked to bring a cake. However, there were a few families in the community who came and ate, and ate but never brought a cake. This made some of the other women angry and they did not hesitate to let everyone know their feelings. But still they came without cakes. But the women who brought cakes baked the best cake they knew how to bake. No one could ever forget the colors of the icing. They were white, red, green, chocolate, pink, yellow, striped, orange, blue and other colors. They made a beautiful display on the kitchen table.

The time to arrive at a cake supper was about dusk, but the cakes were not out until at least ten o'clock. During this time the young people played post office, knock for you lover, or just stood around all armed up and enjoyed the moon and frequent kisses. The older people sat in the house and talked or listened to the music of a fiddle, banjo and guitar. Often some girl sang a solo at the top of her voice which embarrassed her parents and caused everyone to sigh when it was over. But the music was good. They played *Arkansas Traveler, Hell Among the Yearlings, Whiskey Before Breakfast, Missouri Mule, Ragtime Annie,* and dozens of other tunes before the night was over.

The music was played in the kitchen. Anyone knew that music had a better sound when it was played in the kitchen.

During and between tunes the men looked at the cakes on the table and knew that it would not be long until they could eat all they wanted and drink all the coffee in the house.

After they ate, everyone went away happy and well informed with gossip which would last until the next cake supper.

Play Parties

A play party was something like a cake supper except the neighbors took all kinds of food. But much of the food was prepared by the family having the party. While the women were cooking, the men talked about their crops, the weather and any juicy gossip that was going around. The small children were kept in the house and played their games there. But the older ones played party games in the yard or down the lane. Most of the games they played were the same as those played at a music party Now and then a snoopy mother would come out of the house to check on her teenage daughter. She usually didn't look very hard and the games went on.

In the Ozarks a play party was held about once a month. People in the community looked forward to the visiting, the eating and the gossip.

Music Parties

When someone in the community wanted to hear some good music, and maybe dance a little, they announced that someone had decided to have a music party the next Saturday night. People from miles away came. Like the play party and the cake supper, most everyone brought something to eat and the person having the party made some coffee and they ate and listened to the music. Now and then someone's feet began to tickle so they jumped up and did a little jig in one corner of the room. Sometimes these parties lasted until well after midnight.

Songs and Singing and Other Country Music

Many liked to sing and listen to singing. My grandmother sang to me when I was a small boy in the 1930s. Many of the songs she sang came with her from Tennessee and Kentucky shortly after the Civil War.

Mothers and grandmothers would sit on the front porch in the swing and sing. Many sang songs as they worked in the fields or around the house. Many people enjoyed singing at church. I will never forget the solos, quartets and congregational singing.

Singing was so important to the people as a means of entertainment that men who claimed to know something about music notes held singing schools in the community. They could teach the notes but most people knew the songs "by heart" and didn't bother with the notes. Singing school teachers usually charged whatever they could get, usually ten or fifteen cents a lesson. The school usually lasted about fifteen nights so the teacher made a little money.

A few people had a phonograph but they called it a Victrola, which was a brand name. We had one that was my grandmother's "pride and joy." She seemed to enjoy it more than anyone in the family. We kept it going by cranking it before each playing and replacing the needle about once a year.

People traded records, borrowed records, and some bought a few. The following are some I found in Grandma's attic a few years ago.

Melotone Records were manufactured by the Brunswick Recording Company. On one side of the one I found was *Precious Memories* by the McDonald Quartet and on the other side was *Love Lifted Me*.

Columbia Records were manufactured by Columbia Phonograph Company. On one side of one record was *Slow*

Buck by Gid Tanner and his Skillet Lickers with Riley Puckett and Clayton McMichen. On the other side was *Sal Let Me Chew Your Rosin*.

Columbia Records also came out with *We Are Going Down the Valley One by One* by Smith's Sacred Singers. On the other side was *If I'm Faithful to My Lord*.

A 1913 Columbia release that we liked was *What Shall We Do With Mother?* by Rev. M.L. Thrasher and his Gospel Singers. On the other side was *When the Roll is Called up Yonder*.

Brunswick Records recorded *Hear Dem Bells* by Al Hopkins and his Buckle Busters and on side two was *Golden Slippers* by the Kanawha Singers.

Champion Records recorded *What Is It Worth to the Soul* and on side two was *Where the Soul Never Dies*.

Other Champion recordings were *Walking in the Streets of Glory* by George Runnels and Howard Hall. Side two was *He Keeps Me Singing* by the Hutchens Brothers. Another Champion recording that we all liked was *East Bound Train* sung by Jesse Coat and John Bishop and on the other side they recorded *The Old New Hampshire Village*.

Everyone in the neighborhood seemed to enjoy Champion's *Where We Will Never Grow Old* and *Keep Holding On* by the Goodman Sacred Singers.

Champion's *My Loved Ones are Waiting for Me* and *Don't Put Off Salvation Too Long* by the Carolina Ladies Quartette; *My Old Pal* and *Daddy and Home* by Luke Baldwin seemed to be the whole neighborhood's favorites.

Many people in the hills could play a fiddle, banjo, guitar, mandolin, harmonica and an organ. Some could play other instruments. Some who could not afford a real instrument used an OCB or TOP cigarette paper placed over a hair comb. They would blow on the paper and the sound was like a saxophone or other wind instruments or they could use a leaf or place their tongue in a certain position and get the same effect.

My mother and grandmother liked to sit in the porch swing after supper and sing these ballads. When company came, they would take them to the organ inside and they would sing one after the other. If they could find a recording of a song they liked, they bought it or borrowed it from a friend.

Many of these songs were found in songbooks that people had in their bookcases. Some of the folk songs and ballads that were popular in the Ozarks in the nineteenth century and well into the twentieth century are as follows:

- *Missouri Gal*
- *The Baggage Coach Ahead*
- *Little Rosewood Casket*
- *The Drunkard's Child*
- *Sam Bass*
- *The Letter Edged in Black*
- *Chuka, Chuka, Chuka*
- *Mother Shipton's Prophecy*
- *Paddywack*
- *Barbara Allan*
- *My Old Pal*
- *Dear Charlie*
- *Blue Velvet Band*
- *Wild Flowers Don't Care Where They Grow*
- *Bury Me Beneath the Willow*
- *Maple on the Hill*
- *Jimmy Brown*
- *When You and I Were Young, Maggie*

During the Depression time and into the 40s people in the Ozarks liked Jimmie Rodger's songs. They bought his records and were amazed when they heard him yodel. My parents, grandparents and neighbors in Ozark County, Missouri like to hear him sing their favorites as follows:

- *Muleskinner Blues*
- *Blue Yodel No. 1*
- *Waiting for a Train*
- *Daddy and Home*
- *TB Blues*
- *T for Texas*
- *No Hard Time Blues*

They also liked the Carter family and enjoyed hearing them sing many songs including *Keep on the Sunny Side, Little Darling, Pal of Mine* and *Worried Man Blues.*

If the "B" battery or "A" battery for the radio was not too weak, we waited eagerly for the time for the *Grand Ole Opry, National Barn Dance, Renfro Valley Barn Dance* or about any station with music on it.

People in our community learned the "religious" songs at church. Since many people went to church every Sunday and Wednesday prayer meeting and to all the revivals they knew about, they soon learned many songs and sang some of their favorites over and over.

Some of their favorites were as follows:

- *Oh Why Not Tonight*
- *Amazing Grace*
- *Shall We Gather at the River*
- *I'll Fly Away*
- *Love Lifted Me*
- *Just As I Am*
- *Onward Christian Soldiers*
- *Rock of Ages*
- *The Old Rugged Cross*
- *When the Roll is Called Up Yonder*
- *What A Friend*
- *Leaning on the Everlasting Arms*
- *No, Not One*
- *Jesus Hold My Hand*
- *The Lily of the Valley*
- *There is Power in the Blood*
- *I Am Bound for the Promised Land*
- *Old Time Religion*
- *Sweet Hour of Prayer*
- *When We All Get to Heaven*
- *Nearer the Cross*
- *Are You Washed in the Blood*
- *Jesus is Calling*
- *There's A Great Day Coming*
- *Standing on the Promises*
- *The Uncloudy Day*
- *Glory to His Name*
- *Only Trust Him*
- *Almost Persuaded*
- *Old Camp Meetin' Time*

2 Soon 2 Be 4 Gotten

Ozark fiddle players had a large repertoire of tunes. One fiddle player in the Ozarks told me that he knew over 500 tunes. Some of the tunes were played for the two-step, for the waltz, for the square dance and some were "hoedowns" which were good tunes for the square dance and the jig dance.

The following are tunes that I have heard different players play at music parties, dances or maybe just under a shade tree in a "jamming session" during my lifetime.

- Hell Among the Yearlings
- Blackberry Blossom
- Fiddlers Dream
- Walkin' in my Sleep
- Sugar Tree Stomp
- Turkey in the Straw
- Lonesome Indian
- Brown's Dream
- Durham's Bull
- Ragtime Annie
- Arkansas Traveler
- Missouri Mule
- Tennessee Waggoner
- Kickin Mule
- Ruben
- 8th of January
- Cripple Creek
- Black Mountain Rag
- Orange Blossom Special
- Bill Cheatum
- The Two Soldiers
- Fire on the Mountain
- Solder's Joy
- Yellow Rose Waltz
- Golden Slippers
- Shuckin Corn
- Corina
- Bully of the Town
- Flop Eared Mule
- Red Haired Boy
- Lonesome Road Blues
- Mississippi Sawyer
- Old Joe Clark
- Lost Indian
- Whiskey Before Breakfast
- Cotton Eyed Joe
- Sally Goodin
- The Waltz You Saved for Me
- Under the Double Eagle
- Joe Turner Blues
- Milk Cow Blues
- Sally Ann
- Carrol County Blues
- Green Valley Waltz

Reading Material

Hill people liked to read. Even though they had to read by coal oil lamplight, they read. Of course the lamp globe which darkened when the flame of the wick got too high, had to be cleaned often. Usually this was the job of the children to keep it clean. And they had to be careful and not break it for lamp globes were ten to fifteen cents at the store. However, no good housekeeper would allow a soot-coated lamp in the house. The wick had to be watched also. If it got too short, it could cause an explosion if it got too close to the oil. But these chores were taken care of and the reading went on. When the Aladdin Lamp became available, the printed page looked like a new world. This lamp was a prized possession and children were cautioned not to walk too heavily or the mantle of the lamp might fall apart. And when electric lights came to the rural Ozarks in the 1930s, the reader had nothing to do but look for reading material. (Urban areas like Springfield, Missouri had electric lights much earlier than this.)

People did most of their reading during the long, cold winter nights. During other times of the year they were busy working outside. They liked to keep informed about local, county, state and national affairs. If they didn't like the constable, the county assessor, the governor or the president, they wanted to read about what they were doing so they could "give 'em hell."

They read for information, for pleasure and for their children. Parents shared much of what they read with the entire family.

Children liked to read, too. My wife remembers that when she was in grade school that she borrowed a book, *Gone With the Wind*, from a student in another school and read it in a very short time.

When children had the measles, their parents would not let them read for fear it would strain their eyes. My wife remembers her mother putting her in a room that had shades but not darkening shades. So she tacked newspapers over the windows to keep out the light. But my wife liked to read so much that she read the newspapers tacked over the windows.

The favorite reading of people in the Ozarks was the *Bible*, the local county paper, especially the "items" section, *Sears and Roebuck Catalogue*, *Montgomery-Ward Catalogue*, detective magazines, newspapers sold or traded by the peddler and a favorite book they had bought or received as a gift which they read over and over.

My grandmother, Tennessee James Martin, told me she had read the entire *Bible*. Many people, especially women, in the Ozarks read the entire *Bible*. And they read much of it several times because they always took it to church and read from it there. Reading the *Bible* gave them entertainment and satisfaction. They believed it was their obligation to themselves and their families to know God's word. So they read on and on and kept themselves informed about what was happening around them.

The catalogue reached just about every home in the Ozarks. If one ever ordered anything, they seemed to get you on the list and you would get a new catalogue every year. If you didn't have one, you could borrow one from your neighbor if you promised to have it returned in a certain length of time. I can remember my grandmother letting one of the neighbors borrow our catalogue one time. They just kept and kept it for several weeks. This didn't set well with Grandma. She sent them word by my mother that she must have the "book" back immediately for she wanted to order something. Mother got it back but

Grandma said that that was the last time they would ever borrow anything from her.

They liked to read and look at something they wanted. In fact, they called the catalogue the "wishbook." Well that was what it was for the most part. They would read and read and look and wish but they couldn't afford much of the things they had for sale and they had to pay the postage too.

But the people in the first forty years, at least, of this century, could look and want but they had the will-power to buy only what they needed and leave the other alone until they could afford it. That might never happen but the people believed that the things their family had to have must come first. Need had to come before pleasure. Women could make a dress out of a feed sack and let the pretty one in the catalogue go, forever if they needed to.

After the catalogue was out of date and they had received a new one, they took the used one to the outhouse where they continued to be a valuable service to the entire family.

But once in a while there was someone who read and read but didn't quite know what they had read in the catalogue. They were a little confused about what it said.

Uncle Joe Ben's wife had been dead about six months when he decided that he liked the looks of a pretty woman in the "wishbook". She had on a pretty dress priced at $9.95 and she looked nice and had a pretty smile. She wouldn't be bad to have around the house, he thought. So he thought and thought about it. He would pick up the picture of that pretty woman and pretty dress and look at it every day for a week or so. Finally one day he just made out his order, wrote his check, mailed it and waited. He just waited and thought more and more about that pretty woman in the catalogue. In a few weeks the dress came just like they said it would but there was no woman with it. Uncle Joe Ben was disappointed to say the least. He thought he had ordered the dress and the woman. He got mad and some folks said he began to talk about it and threatened to write the company for false advertising. But some of his neighbors talked to him and explained that the woman didn't go with the dress and that he could send the dress back if he didn't want to keep it and get his money back. So, that is what he did. But he had enjoyed reading about that situation and was glad to have the catalogue around to read even if he couldn't order a good lookin' woman like that in the picture.

One time in northern Arkansas a woman called another woman on the local telephone line and asked her if she would be interested in reading a letter she had got from a man in a distant city. She said it was such good reading that she just had to share it with someone, especially a good friend. She explained that it was just like reading one of them romance stories in a romance magazine. She said it was interesting, so interesting that one could not put it down but would just read it over and over. And, of course, this made the other woman crazy to read it so she just jumped at the chance to read something like that and said she would come over after it. This was, however, uncommon because few people liked for others to read their private letters, especially if they were love letters like she said this one was. Usually, they would put them in a safe hiding place and read them as often as they wanted to.

Some people even wrote letters to just anyone so maybe they would get one in return someday and have something to read.

Another type of reading that people, especially women,

did was reading their own diaries. They were highly secret and no one was allowed to even touch the diary much less read from it. But the person who had written in it enjoyed getting into it and reading whatever they enjoyed. They would then put it back or lock it and never get it out until they wanted to read some part of it again or make another entry in it.

Farm men and women and even their children liked to read veterinarian books. They had the symptoms and recommended treatment for just about any disease that a cow, horse, goat, or chicken might have. Some men of the community read the book so much and did what it said for themselves and their neighbor's livestock that they became pretty good at what they did and called themselves a veterinarian. They were people in demand in the community because there were no certified people like this for miles. So they read the book and usually brought it with them when they came to examine and doctor a sick calf. Sometimes even if the farm family didn't have any problem with any of their livestock or chickens, they just read the book for information or for pleasure.

No one in rural areas had extra money to buy magazines like detective magazines so if someone in the community had one somehow, they passed it around from family to family and they read it from cover to cover. If a story was going to be written about a murder in another state close by like Kansas, someone would find out about it in some way and have someone send them the detective magazine which they would read and pass around. The murder mysteries that appeared in these magazines were the most popular. People in the Ozarks wanted to know about murders, it seemed, so they would know what to look out for if anyone came through their "neck of the woods" with robbery and murder on their minds. They believed the story would give them some good information and some good reading.

One of the most popular publications of Ozark readers in the 20s was the *Comfort* paper. Some called it the "Comfort Magazine". It was published by W. H. Gannett Publishers of Augusta, Maine. It was published monthly at a cost of 50¢ for a year's subscription in 1920.

My grandmother seemed to keep all the copies that she received. She read each copy carefully and would often go back to her stack of papers and re-read. She must have enjoyed the August 1920 issue for it survived for eighty years, along with some others. There is no wonder she liked this paper for it contained short stories, recipes, advertisements of all kinds, a discussion of how to raise poultry, almost a full page on farming, a column that young girls could send letters and ask questions, a page devoted to manners, information about veterinary questions, a page that gave legal information and one that gave medical advice from a doctor.

Like books these papers were passed around in the neighborhood for everyone to read and then talk about. But most people who shared the paper were like Grandma. They wanted them back in a few days and they wanted them returned in good condition. If they were not, everyone heard about it on the local telephone the next few days. It was interesting to listen to people talk about the information they got from the *Comfort*.

Another publication, *The Illustrated Companion or a Journal of Illustrative Literature for the Home* was also popular during the early part of the century. It was published by F. B. Warner Company of New York City. It was a monthly publication. The price was 50¢ a year or four years for a dollar.

In the October 1926 issue several interesting stories were included, along with many interesting advertisements, a column called "Cupid's Corner" and another called "The Children's Corner." People of the Ozarks enjoyed a page of want-ads. But most of all they enjoyed the advertisements. Just about anything was on the market to help people in some way.

Grandma kept all the papers of this type that she got, just like she did the *Comfort*. She just stacked them neatly in a stack by themselves alphabetically by month and year. This way she could get a copy in a hurry.

These two papers, the *Comfort* and *The Illustrated Companion* provided much entertainment and joy to people, especially elderly women who liked to read and wish for something as they read the advertisements. Many long, cold winter nights became shorter as the whole family sat around the fireplace and discussed what they would like to have in the advertisements or how good or bad a character was in one of the stories.

Since doctors were hard to get to come to a rural house in the mountains, people in the Ozarks were interested in the advertisements of salves, tonics and medicines for infections. If they could order something advertised in these two papers that would keep their back from hurting, make a cut on their body heal faster, or help the children with kidney and bladder problems, they told everyone they saw about it and soon it became popular. A satisfied customer was good advertising for many things that they ordered. People of the Ozarks liked to talk about things that made them feel better, whether it was from the fields and woods or from some company in a far away city.

From the time before the Civil War and well into the 1930s there were not many books available in rural areas.

Schools had a few books, especially for children and adults. A majority of homes had few, if any, books but if they had only one book, it was a great possession and was kept in a safe place where nothing would soil it and book markers were used religiously. There was always a fear that mice or rats would destroy a book so they were kept in a place that would make them safe from such things. To keep the pages clean and in good condition, children were taught how to turn pages correctly. They were taught this at home and at school.

My grandfather, Jonathan Decker, of near Dora, Missouri, had a favorite book, *The Royal Path of Life or Aims to Success and Happiness* which he brought with him to Missouri from Kentucky shortly after the Civil War.

It was written by T.L. Haines and L.W. Yaggy and published by Southwestern Publishing Company of Nashville, Tennessee in 1876. It contained several chapters such as "Life," "Home Influence," "Habit," "Envy," "Vanity," "Anger," and "Pride."

Another book that people in the Ozarks seemed to like was the *Golden Censer or Duties of Today and Hopes of the Future*. It was written by John McGovern of the *Chicago Tribune* and published by Union Publishing Company of Chicago in 1883. It contained such chapters as "Home," "Prudence in Speech," and "Duties of Parents."

It seemed that many people liked to gain all the knowledge they could from books like the two just mentioned and the *Bible*. This interest in this type of reading would lead one to think that the people wanted to do the best for themselves, for their families and for their fellow man.

Since there were few books, children and adults alike took care of books. They borrowed books and had respect enough for the book and the person from whom they borrowed it to take care of it. A person had to be a very good friend to borrow a book from someone.

Many have told me that some of their favorite books were *The Legend of Sleepy Hollow, The Spy, The Last of the Mohicians, The Deerslayer, The Red Badge of Courage, The Scarlet Letter, Tom Sawyer, Huck Finn, Uncle Remus, Rebecca of Sunnybrook Farm* and *The Shepherd of the Hills*.

People on all sides of my family were serious readers. When I was growing up in the 30s and 40s, they would mention these books and let me know that if I got a good education, I would need to read these books and many more.

Tricksters

To play a trick on a neighbor was a thrill to some several years ago. Although many of the tricks were rather crude and dangerous, it was a means of great entertainment and gave many a person a hearty laugh.

One story of a trick is about a group of people in southern Missouri who got together one night and began to think about a way they could have some fun. It did not take long for them to agree on a plan. They got all the ropes and chains they could find and marched down the road to an elderly man's house. It was late at night and the man and his wife had gone to bed. They yelled at the yard gate. The man and his wife were hard to wake so they yelled louder and louder until they saw a light from the man's lamp. They continued to yell like something was urgent or like someone was hurt. Finally, after looking out the window to see what was going on, the man and his wife opened the front door and looked out and saw twenty-five or thirty of their neighbors standing outside in the moonlight.

"George," they said, "your cow has fallen in the well. Tell your wife to help you find as many ropes and chains as you can and come to the well. We'll try to help you get her out. We have ropes and chains but more will help. Now hurry."

The old man and his wife had very little of anything so they became very excited for fear their only cow, Daisy, that gave them milk would be hurt or dead.

They ran frantically about the house in the dark looking for anything that they thought would help get the cow out of the well.

Now Uncle George and his wife had just finished digging the well at the back of their house a few days before so they thought it could be possible that their cow had fallen in, since she did not know it was there.

Soon they came out to the gate where the neighbors were standing. Everyone had plenty of chains and ropes so they started for the back of the house where the well was located. As they went toward the well, chains clattered and neighbors said in low voices how bad it was to have lost the cow and spoiled the well all at one time. Uncle George and his wife could be heard moaning about their misfortune.

When they got to the well, of course, there was no cow in it. At first the old man looked relieved but soon he began to curse everything and everybody. The tricksters laughed at every sound he made. The more he cursed the more they laughed. Finally, Uncle George saw that his cursing was not doing any good so he just joined the tricksters and began to laugh too.

After everyone laughed for awhile, Uncle George and his wife invited everyone into the house for some coffee and tea. They built a fire in the fireplace, drank their tea and coffee and now and then someone would burst out laughing about the trick they had just pulled on their good neighbor.

Finally about midnight the tricksters decided it was time to go. They had had their fun for the night. After they went on their way the old man and his wife blew out the lights and tried to get a good night's sleep.

Preachers who came to communities in southern Missouri and northern Arkansas to hold revival meetings were often the objects of local tricksters. My grandfather told me about a good revival that was going on in his community. Although it was in August and hot and dry, the church house was full just about every night for two weeks. But about the middle of the revival some young boys in their teens and, some said, several adult men in their twenties, slipped into the attic of the church house before meetin' time and set a bucket of cold water above a hole in the ceiling just above where the preacher was likely to be standing most of the time during the evening service. They tied a small rope or cord to the handle of the bucket and ran the other end of the cord out the back of the building. One trickster hid close enough to a window to watch the preacher, and the others stood behind the church house and held the end of the cord. When the preacher brought his sermon to its highest point, the boy at the window gave a sign to the boys holding the cord behind the building. They pulled the cord and the bucket of water came down on the poor preacher. Of course this stopped his sermon because his attention was interrupted and the elders and deacons ran outside to find who had done such an ungodly act. But by this time the tricksters had run into the dark woods and were safe. Some people said that the elders and deacons were chasing some of their own kids but this was never known in the community.

After everyone came back in and the preacher got dried off, the sermon turned to this being a good example of the works of the devil and how sinful it was for a community to allow something like this to happen, especially to a visiting preacher.

Sometimes when the boys were feelin' a little meaner they put tar and feathers in the bucket instead of water. They used the same method of pulling the bucket over when the time was right; this was worse than the water. The tar got all on the preacher's shirt which was usually a white one and in his hair if he had any and dripped down on the floor. It dripped freely because in hot weather the tar got hot in the attic of the church house and become thin so it ran easily. This made most preachers madder than when water came down because the tar was so messy and it just kept drippin' down from the ceiling. Some man in the community was talkin' about a trick like this that had been played the night before at the revival. He talked seriously about it but finally laughed a little and said, "Well, you know all that tar comin' down so unexpected is enough to make a preacher cuss."

Sometimes in the 1930s and before the preacher rode a horse to the revival meeting. A favorite trick was to grease the saddle or smear it with wet paint. A slick saddle made the riding uneven and could cause the rider to fall off the horse.

Another trick was to slip out to the place the preacher had his horse tied and change the saddle by putting it on backwards. When the poor preacher came from the church filled with the glory of a good sermon and many tight handshakes from the good sisters and jumped into a saddle and found himself facing the horse's rear, he was in no mood to continue his meditation.

Of course, the tricksters were hiding nearby watching the entire situation with laughter.

Ozark tricksters thought of everything it seemed. One time an elderly man named Drew had a bunch of sheep that he sheared. After shearing time he placed the wool in sacks in his barn loft. Once just after he had sheared his sheep he told a man about the good neighbors he had in the community. Rist Nubbins was his favorite byword. "Rist Nubbins, these are the best neighbors in the world. No one needs to worry about anything. Best people in the world and honest too."

During this conversation they decided to go out to the barn and look at the fine wool he had stored there a few days before. But when they got there, they could not find the wool. The wool was gone. They looked everywhere but there was no wool. It was then that the man began to wonder about his neighbors.

Actually, a group of tricksters in the neighborhood had taken the wool and placed it in the loft of a man's shop. One of the tricksters just happened to come by while they were going from the barn past the neighbor's shop. He looked up and whispered to the man, "Look, there is Drew's wool."

This caused much confusion and ill feeling in the community but the tricksters had had their fun. After a day or so the men who were involved in the trick told Mr. Drew what they had done.

"Rist Nubbins," he said. "I knew something funny was goin' on. I knew that none of you would steal my wool. I told my wife that no one around here would steal it. But rist nubbins, I didn't think about you takin' the time to move it. Rist nubbins, I didn't."

Dogs and cats had a rough time in the Ozarks if tricksters wanted to have fun with them. Men and boys were so hungry for what was funny to them that they would catch a cat or dog, and one person would hold its head while the other rubbed the tail with a corn cob and then rubbed turpentine on it. Then they would turn the animal loose and they would run until they were out of sight, screaming as they ran. This is the reason that people in the Ozarks refer to some person being in a hurry as "Going as fast as a turpentined cat."

If two tomcats caused too much trouble in a community, people knew how to make them behave and have a little fun too. They would tie the tails of the cats together with a small cord and place them over a clothesline and watch them fight. They would take one end of the line down before they hurt themselves but it was entertainment.

To tie a firecracker to a cat's tail and light it was great fun to many tricksters. The cat would run as fast as it could because of the noise of the fuse of the cracker and when the thing exploded, the cat would jump a mile high in the air. Some people who have done this trick to a poor cat say that in many cases the cat did not return.

In addition to playing pranks on cats and dogs, some people liked to frighten horses and cows. The method they liked best for this was putting white sheets over their heads and running after the horse or cow. These animals would run for dear life and probably tear down any fence they came to.

In Ozark County near Gainesville, Missouri, a man was employed to take care of the cemetery. In the summer he cut the grass. In the fall he raked the leaves and did what was needed the rest of the year. He was a good worker and everyone in the community seemed satisfied with his work.

But as it was in every community, young boys, twelve to seventeen years old, liked to pull tricks on anyone they thought of.

A river ran along one side of this graveyard and in several places there was a high bank from the river to the top where the graves were located. Three of the boys found a piece of pipe about one inch in diameter. They pushed the pipe from the high bank near the river through dirt and grass to the area where graves were located. The pipe that extended into the graveyard could not be seen. Even the end was not visible because the boys made sure it was in an area that would not be disturbed.

When the man came to that area to rake leaves that fall, the boys were behind the riverbank not very far from him but in a place that they would not be seen. As the man raked, the boys spoke into the end of the pipe. "Don't rake leaves off my grave," came the voice from among the graves.

At first the man only stopped for a moment and then went back to raking leaves. The boys waited about five minutes and spoke again. "Don't rake leaves off my grave," came the voice again. This time it was just too much for the man. He threw down his rake and ran as hard as he could out of the graveyard and on to his own home. He swore he would never set foot in that place again.

This story was told to me by Frank McClendon of Gainesville, Missouri.

One may wonder how the boys knew the way the man reacted since they were all behind the high bank out of sight. Well, as in most cases they had a lookout who watched it all from a distance and probably had more fun than the boys.

Snipe hunting was a trick played near Halloween time.

2 Soon 2 Be 4 Gotten

In one-room schools in the Ozarks the teacher would announce one day that as a treat the children could go snipe hunting. A snipe is a rather large bird, yet smaller than a crow, with a long bill. It lives in marshland areas. Its color is dark brown or almost black.

The children who had never been on a snipe hunt were told to go to the mouth of a hollow and hold open a gunny sack and catch a snipe as it came down the hollow. They were told that the rest of the students who knew something about this type of hunting would go to the head of the hollow and drive the snipes down to those who were going to catch them.

After the students who were holding the sacks were positioned, the others went back to the schoolhouse and played games while they waited for those trying to catch the snipes. If they did not come in after an hour or two, the teacher rang the school bell and the poor students came back with their sacks but no snipes. They were embarrassed that they had fallen for such a trick. But it was fun and they looked forward for new students the next year so they could do the driving and the new students could hold the sacks.

Margaret Evans Frazier of Thornfield, Missouri told me this trick that was told to her by an elderly gentleman in the Pondfork, Missouri area.

It was the annual church association time and people from the community and surrounding areas had come to hear fine preaching and singing. Many of the services were held at night and since it was hot in the buildings, parents put their children to bed in their wagons before they went on inside the church building.

One night someone got the idea that it would be fun to play a trick on the parents who had left their children in the wagons. So they went to each wagon and switched all the babies and little ones to different wagons. Now church association meetings often lasted well into the night so people got home late. This time when they got home, they carried the children from the wagons to put them to bed only to find out that they were not their children.

It was late, hot and dark and they had the wrong child or children. So they had to travel all over the country in the dead of night trying to find their own. Some had to go to several homes before they found their children. Some met others on the road looking for their children. Some looked all night. It was a mess but it was a lot of fun and entertainment for the tricksters.

Pop Ramsey of Mountain View, Arkansas, told me that this trick was pulled on about everyone who got married around there. As the bride and groom were about to leave the church or wherever they got married, someone would lift their Model-T and put the back tires in fresh cut watermelon rinds. The car would not move. It just set there and its wheels would spin around and around.

Tricksters had a lot of fun with something they made called a "dumb-brough" (Pictured below at right). It was made by stretching the dried skin of a wild animal like the possum or groundhog over the opened end of a nail keg. Then a string was tied to the skin. Next the string was rubbed with rosin. Then the trickster pulled their fingers over the string. This made a terrible sound like the screaming of a wild animal or a wild animal in terrible pain. It

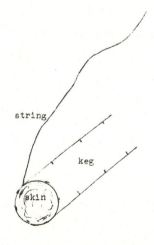

could be heard for at least one-half mile. People used it if they wanted to scare a neighbor, cattle, horses, dogs or cats on a dark night. This trick was told to me by Jim Thurman who grew up in the Sweden, Missouri area but now lives in Ava, Missouri.

A "tic-tac" was similar to the "dumb-brough." A lady who lives near Seymour, Missouri, told me that "old-timers" in the Ozarks used this thing called "tic-tac" to scare anyone they wanted to scare. It gave off the sound of a panther, sounds that came from haunted houses or sounds like wild animals in terrible pain or filled with anger, ready to attack.

According to the lady there were three ways to make one:

One was to take an oatmeal box and punch a hole in the bottom. Then put a string through the hole. To keep the string in place, tie the end to a short stick. Then they put rosin on the string and pulled it through their fingers.

Another method was a little more complicated. They would drill a hole in the bottom of a cedar churn and put a cat gut string through the hole. Next they tied the end of the string to a short piece of wood to hold it secure. Then they put rosin on the string and pulled it through the fingers.

To make a loud, terrible noise in a house, they put a small piece of cedar shingle under the weatherboard of a house. Then they attached a string to it and brought it through an oatmeal box. Then they put rosin on the string and pulled it through the fingers.

This "tic-tac" trick is effective if one wanted to scare someone late at night or on a dark Halloween night.

One major advantage of both the "tic-tac" and the "dumb-brough" was the fact that the trickster could be several hundred yards away from their victim. So they were less likely to get caught.

Tricksters often focused their attention on the one-room country school teacher. During the Christmas season the local school teacher always had a Christmas program. They were expected to have one. At the end of the program which was usually held on Friday afternoon before Christmas, the teacher treated the children with large sacks of candy with an apple or an orange. And, they always had a large box, all they could carry, of treats for the parents or any other person who was not in school but who had come to the Christmas program.

Most of the adults were nice and considerate and took only the amount of candy they could eat. And some didn't take that much. But on one occasion some boys who had been out of school for two or three years took more than their share. They reached in the box and took out double handfuls and put it in the pockets of their coats or anywhere they could think of to store it. Well, the teacher who was passing the candy around tried to go on to the next person but they just kept taking it out by the handfuls. Finally he did get to move on with his box but it was too late. He soon ran out of candy before he got to everybody.

There were several people who got no treats at all. And it just happened that those he didn't get to were there only for the treats and not for the program. In fact, many of them had come in just for the treats and hadn't watched the program. So they grumbled about the tight teacher who would not buy enough candy for the people who came to their program. It was not good local school politics to run out that way, but the teacher hadn't expected some of them to take so much.

Jokes and Short Stories

People liked to hear good jokes and they liked to tell

them. It seemed that some people could just do a better job telling a joke than other people. A good joke teller told his joke slowly and made sure that the "punch line" came at the right time. Men were careful not to tell a rather vulgar joke before children or in the presence of women. Of course, their definition of vulgar could be questioned at times. But usually they were gentlemen when it came to telling a joke.

Many jokes were uproariously funny. Some were "made-up." But many were like short stories told and retold because they liked to tell stories about certain people.

No one knows where jokes got started. Some people who moved into a community brought jokes with them. But they didn't "take" in the new community even if they applied to a local resident. To be a good joke for that community, it had to start there and be about someone who lived there or had lived there.

Like gossip, jokes changed from one telling to the next. But they had the same appeal. They made people laugh and have fun and the teller felt good that they had made someone laugh. And a good joke or storyteller laughed at their own stories and jokes and that made them feel good.

In small towns the barbershop was the place to hear a good joke. Or, even if the barber was cutting hair under a shade tree, and several men were loafing there, it was quite possible that someone would tell a joke and it would go from there.

Swiney Rayfield who lives near Eminence in Shannon County, Missouri, told me several jokes and stories that have been told in his "neck of the woods" for some time.

He remembered a barber who cut hair for 25¢ and gave a good shave for a dime and usually added a little goodsmellin' lotion after the shave. The men around Eminence liked his shaves. They felt good walkin' around town with a nice smooth face.

One day one of the men of the town was in the chair getting a shave. There were several loafing in the shop. One of his friends spoke to the barber.

The loafer said, "Don't put any of that sweet smelling stuff on him. His wife will think he has been in a whorehouse."

"No, go on and put it on," the man in the chair said, "My wife doesn't know what a whorehouse smells like."

Another man came into the shop that afternoon who didn't have much hair, just a little ring just above his ears. The rest of his head was just slick, shiny skin. The barber rubbed his hand over the skin. Just kept rubbing his hand over the soft skin. As he kept on rubbing he said, "That feels just like my wife's butt."

The man in the chair took his own hand and rubbed it over the bald area of his head several times and said, "Yeah, by gosh, it does!"

The loafers in the shop roared with laughter and told the barber that he ought to keep a watch on his wife and his customers. And they laughed and talked about this for months. Got a lot of enjoyment out of it.

During the early part of the century most all small towns had their share of drunks. Swiney remembers hearing about a man in Eminence, Missouri who was drunk every day. He was an alcoholic. One day a medical doctor friend to the man said to him, "You are going to kill yourself. You don't eat. You just drink. People walk all over you as they go down the street. All you do is drink. You're going to kill yourself."

The old drunk answered him slowly, "Don't worry

about it. There's lots of old drunks around here but not many doctors."

There was a man in Shannon County who was a good horse and cow doctor. He was not a veterinarian, just someone who knew something about animals. He didn't charge much, maybe a peck of potatoes or something like that. One day he was called to a place where a man had a cow that was sick and down. The doctor worked on her and went on his way. The next morning the owner of the cow saw the man in town and told him that his cow had died that night.

"I knew she would," said the doctor.

"Well, why in the hell did you doctor her then?"

The doctor replied, "That's why you called me, wasn't it."

Back in the 30s a man in Shannon County was charged for murder for killing his neighbor. It all came about when the man shot and killed the man's dog. The man who owned the dog shot the man who had killed his dog. It came to court and was tried before a judge from that area. He listened to the evidence and didn't take long to return his verdict. He set the man free.

"Anyone who kills a man's dog ought to be killed himself," the judge said.

The history of this trial was given to me by Swiney Rayfield who emphasized that in that part of the Ozarks a man's dog was like a member of the family and no one mistreated another man's dog.

For many years people, residents and tourists have enjoyed standing on the bridge at Eminence, Missouri and watching the Jacks Fork River. It is a peaceful environment that most people would agree that God gave some special attention.

During the Depression a man from this area went to Kansas to work in the wheat. He worked long enough to buy a small plot of land. He continued to work hard, raised more wheat and as he made more money, he bought more land until he had several sections after several years.

Swiney Rayfield said he came back to the area around Eminence for a visit. One of the first places he went was to look at the beautiful water of the Jacks Fork as it passed through town. While he was viewing the river from the bridge, he "struck up" a conversation with one of the residents who had not left the area but stayed and had come through the Depression.

"I don't see how you made a living around here. Looks like you would have starved to death. Now out in Kansas there is money everywhere from the wheat. You can just see oceans of money as the wheat moves with the wind. There's just money everywhere."

"Yeah," the old-timer said. "You may have all that wheat and it makes all that money but you don't have this water like we are lookin' at her in Jacks Fork. You don't have that."

"Well, maybe not," said the man from Kansas. "But I've made enough money that I could have all this water piped out there. No problem. No problem at all. I've got the money and I can do it."

"I don't think all that would be necessary," the old-timer said.

"If you can suck as well as you can blow, I think you could just suck all this water out there."

Swiney told me that men from this area went to Jefferson Barracks in St. Louis to be examined for the armed services during World War II.

When the boys from Shannon County got there, the

officers would say, "Well here's some more boys from Shannon County. Better give them a search."

Some would have a knife with a blade a little too long or a bottle of whiskey in their pocket.

He remembered one young man who went to St. Louis for his examination, but in a few day he came back home. He said they would not take him because he had literacy.

Some of the folks he was talking to said, "You mean they said you were illiterate."

"Yes, that's what they said and I told them that wasn't so cause my parents were married three or four years before I was born. They said up there in St. Louis just to go on back home and nobody would ever know I had it."

Situations like this happened in most counties in the Ozarks. But when these men got in the army, they were good, tough fighters who were excellent with a rifle. They had had plenty of practice shooting gray squirrels as they jumped from tree to tree. They had plenty of experience with a 22 rifle and a larger gun didn't bother them.

My father, E.C. Decker (1895-1990), was a good joke and storyteller. He told a few to me but I slipped around and heard many others that he was telling some of the neighbors, usually at the country store.

He seemed to enjoy telling a story about a farmer in Wright County, Missouri near Mtn. Grove who was shopping for a car one time during the 1930s. So the car salesman took him for a ride. They were going about as fast as the car would run when they saw a railroad track ahead, with warning lights blinking. The car salesman hit the brakes and they came to a stop only a few feet from the tracks as the train went by like the wind. In the process the salesman had applied the brakes so hard that they had scorched and smelled.

"Smell that, old boy," the salesman said in an attempt to call attention to the good workable brakes on the car.

"Smell hell," said the farmer. "I'm settin' in it."

He told another story that happened near Mtn. Grove, Missouri. Two young men came along about time for church. After a short time they decided to go in, and found that the members of the church were taking the sacrament. They were rather mean young men so when the "cup" was passed to them, they drank all of it.

Most men in the hills liked to tell and hear a joke about sex. This story was told in many communities but it was one of my dad's favorites. Someone asked a ninety-year-old man when sex became less important to a person.

"You'll have to ask someone older than me," he said.

During the Depression a man and his neighbor near Elijah, Missouri had worked in the log woods all day. They were hot and tired. One man said to the other. "Here we are workin', tired and hungry and that President up there in Washington has all the cheese and crackers he can eat."

I heard my dad telling this story at a picnic one time. It seems that churches in a community were always having to make decisions. During a business meeting at one church sometime in the 30s the preacher suggested to the members that they should bring axes and cut the elders near the church. Well, one sister didn't quite understand what they were talking about and she couldn't hear too well either. So she said, "Now, I believe if you are going to cut the elders, you ought to cut the deacons too."

My dad didn't live far from Trail, Missouri where one time a man was asked to take a woman to the doctor because she was about to have a baby. They couldn't get the doctor to come all the way from Dora, Missouri to deliver the baby, although it wasn't all that far. So they had to call an old farmer to deliver the baby as they were trying to get to the doctor.

Someone said, "John Henry, what did you do when you had that woman in the wagon and she had her baby?"

"Well," John Henry said, with a nervous crack in his voice. "I didn't do much until after it was born. Then I took my old rusty knife and cut the little feller's naval string. I hear he's doing pretty good."

Many stories were told about moonshiners who were people who made whisky especially during Prohibition. They often selected a deep "holler" so they could not be seen easily by "revenuers." That was a good place to set up their still. One time while making "shine" not far from Rockbridge, Missouri, the men started sampling their product as they always did. But this time it seemed that they sampled it too much too long. When it came time to leave, they could not climb the steep path that led up the hill out of the "holler." One big man got almost to the place that he could go over the top of the ridge but each time he got near the top he was so drunk that he slipped back down. One man in the group was a little man who was not quite so drunk. He put his shoulder next to the big man's rear and gradually pushed him over after several tries. (Another good reason to have the still in a deep hollow was so they could have plenty of spring water.)

Baxter Gaulding who lived in Gainesville, Nottinghill and Ava, Missouri told me a story about something that happened when he lived near Nottinghill. It seems that two men were traveling through the country and decided to stop and rest at the farmer's house. So they sat down on the front porch with the farmer and his son. As they talked, one of the men said he needed to go to the bathroom and headed off in the direction of a dug well that had just filled with clean, pure water. Naturally the farmer was fearful of what might happen. He yelled at the top of his voice.

He yelled, "Stop him! Stop him! Hit him in the head with a rock!"

Baxter Gaulding told this story on himself. He said that a neighbor sent his son to his house to borrow some blueing. When he asked to borrow the blueing, jolly Mr. Gaulding said, "Sure, what color do you want?"

He also told about chores that boys and girls had to do each morning and night in the Ozarks. One of his chores at night was to go to the dug well and turn the chickens. It seemed that they liked to roost on the top of the well so he had to turn them so their heads would be pointed in.

He lived through the Depression and had many stories and jokes about it. One story that he told was about someone seeing a man coming out of a burning house with one shoe on.

Someone said, "Jake, did you lose your shoe?"

Jake said, "No, I found one."

He emphasized that people in the Ozarks didn't get in much of a hurry about anything. He said that sometime in the 1920s a man was resting himself on his front porch. He looked down the road and saw one of his neighbors coming slowly toward his house. The neighbor after several minutes came up to the house and very slowly said to the man on the porch, "Bob, your house in on fire."

My Uncle Eldon Decker who lived at Dora, Missouri most of his life told me that people in the Ozarks were independent even if it meant losing something that they liked very much. He told about one of his neighbors who was sent to prison. When he went in the prison, they took all his possessions, and of course his knife. But when he served his time, less than a year, the prison officials brought his personal possessions that they had kept for him. Among them was a knife.

"That's not my knife," he said.

So the prison official brought out dozens of knives, much better than the one he had had at first. Again he told them that none of these were his knife.

"But take any one you want," the prison official said.

"No, if I can't have my knife, you can take these and go to HELL," he said and left without any knife.

My uncle also told me about a man in the Ozarks who learned that his wife who was about forty-five years old was pregnant. The next day he was at the country store telling the boys about it. "Yeah, when she told me, I thought I'd just go shoot myself. Then I got to thinking. No, I better not do that. I might be killing an innocent man."

Sometime in the early 1940s four men from a community in southern Missouri all had some business in Jefferson City, Missouri; so they all decided to go together to cut down on expenses. And they thought that since they were all good friends they would enjoy the ride together. To enhance their enjoyment, they bought a quart of good Kentucky whiskey before they left. And not many miles up the road they began to do some sipping. As they traveled on, one man in the front seat thought it would be interesting to the others and especially to him to talk about his wealth. He told about his land holdings, about several rental buildings he had in a small town, about the large number of cattle he had and how much money he had in the bank. This went on for some time when one of the men in the back seat who had not had quite as much to drink said to the man in the front seat, "Boys, pass that bottle back here again. I think one more drink and I'll be out of debt."

As I have mentioned in another section of this book, people in the Ozarks liked to read. Jim Thurman of Ava, Missouri told me about a man he knew when he lived in Houston, Missouri who saw an advertisement in the paper and ordered him a wife from Mississippi. She arrived in a few days and he kept her for a few weeks but decided she didn't have any money and wouldn't work very much so he bought her a bus ticket and sent her back south. He said as she left, "It's a poor hen that can't scratch for two chickens."

My grandfather Jonathan Decker of Birdtown, Missouri seemed to know thousands of stories and jokes. He told me about a man in the Ozarks who was about ninety years old but did not have any white hair. Someone asked him how it stayed so black, not a gray hair in sight.

"Well, every time I get a haircut, I bury my hair. This is supposed to keep it from getting gray, I am told."

He knew a man who was so stingy that he wouldn't buy gum to chew but instead wound up strings to chew.

People in the Ozarks liked to make up rhymes that were often "off color" just a little. Since Grandpa had a store, maybe this happened to him:

I had a little monkey
And I took him to the store.
He "peed" on the counter
And he "peed" on the floor.

Grandpa said that people in these hills liked to tell stories about rural schools and teachers. Once such story was about an arithmetic problem. The teacher told a student that to find the circumference of a circle that they should square the (r) radius times the (pi). The student did not understand. They argued that (pi) (r) round. Cornbread (r) square.

Most rural farmhouses had rain barrels to catch water as it ran off the roof of the house. This was called "soft" water and was good for washing clothing and ones hair. One time a woman detected an odor and somewhat of a strange color in her water. She was mad and accused some neighbor boys of pissin' in her barrel. That caused the boy's parents to become angry at the woman and threatened to slip to the house every time the barrel got full and turn it over. The feud went on for several years until both sides got tired of it and turned their attention to something else.

Grandpa told this story about a man in the community who was a drunk. One night he came home drunk. He had done this several times before and his wife and kids and several of the women of the community were tired of it. So the neighbor women went over and they talked about the problem and decided to help the family anyway they could. They all stayed until he came home and fell into bed drunk. While he was there in the bed, they took white shoe polish and put it all over his hair. The next morning when he finally woke up, and looked in the mirror, he saw his white hair. The neighbors and his wife told him his hair had turned white because he had been so drunk the night before and that he had aged at least twenty years. So he vowed to never take a drink again.

People in the hills seem to have difficulty letting go of traditions. My grandparents raised six boys and a girl. After the children were grown and gone, Grandma set her table as if they were all there. The long table looked strange. Grandma set at one end and Grandpa at the other. In between were seven place settings.

My mother, Gladys Martin Decker, told me that not everyone could become a resident of a community in the Ozarks. She said that a local newspaper reported a man's death as follows: "He was ninety-eight years old. Although he was not a resident of this town, he had lived here since he was three years old."

She said that hill people believed in giving proper warning to everyone who might be getting into trouble. If a person found a bundle of switches on their front door step, they knew someone was saying that they were doing something wrong and better stop. Sometimes community leaders did this to a man or even a woman.

My grandmother, Tennessee James Martin, told me many stories about things that happened during the Depression. One story was about a woman who papered her walls with newspapers. They looked strange but they were clean and neat. This showed the pride people had even if their house might have been a crude log house.

This same lady who papered her walls with newspapers was very clean and if you went there, she would ask you in with this statement: "Come in if you can get in for the dirt."

My grandmother said that many people in the hills liked to give their child a nickname. Once, a little boy was ready to start to school. All his life his parents and everyone had called him by his nickname. Before school started, his mother had told him that at school they would want to know his real name, not just his nickname. So the first day of school came and the little boy started down the lane to the school. His parents were there to tell him goodbye. As he walked on, he suddenly stopped and yelled back to his parents and said, "Mama, what did you say my name was?"

My wife, Mona Gaulding Decker, said that the people around Hammond, Missouri who were going to have a play party, would wait until four or five o'clock and make a trip around the community and invite who they wanted.

People were creative in the hills. My wife told me about having her folks cut the bottom of cans that fruit came in so they could be used in a playhouse store. As a child, she also made mud pies out of red clay and to add an extra coating on top, she sprinkled the red clay with black dirt.

Growing up in the Ozarks and living here all my life has given me the opportunity to observe many events and to hear many stories and jokes that I can't remember the source, and to have experienced many things.

I saw a sign in an Ozark Mountain café that was closed. It read SHUT.

Friends give me a buckeye about ever year. They believe if anyone carries one, they will have good luck. Sometimes I just pick some off the trees where they grow.

In these mountains on election years about all candidates show up at funerals. If they are not candidates that year, they seem less likely to come. But it is good politics to be there and they know it. And people who have lost loved ones expect it. This is something that people use as stories when they talk about an election and who may win or lose.

This is a true story that happened to me in 1938 near Lawndale, Missouri in Ozark County. In the 30s and 40s people went to "shade-tree" barbers to get their hair cut for twenty-five cents. They were called "shade-tree" barbers because they put you on a stool under a shade tree and cut your hair. This barber was cutting my hair and had one side just about done. He cut one side and then another.

About this time he heard a truck coming down the hill to take a calf to West Plains, Missouri to the market. So he dropped everything, loaded the calf and went with the truck driver to town to sell the calf. So I went home with my hair cut on one side but not on the other. He was a very independent barber. I didn't go anywhere that night and went back the next day and got the other side done. I remember looking in the mirror that night and almost crying because I did look terrible.

People in the Ozarks have always been known for their friendliness. One day my daughter and I were passing a house and saw a man carrying an armload of stove wood. When we waved at him, he threw down his wood and waved back. From then on, every time we passed his house near Three Brothers, Arkansas we looked to see if he was anywhere around to give us a wave.

As I fished the North Fork of White River when I was a boy, I always remembered the advice old fishermen had given me. They would say if you catch a "water dog" or "mud puppy" in a fishing hole, you might as well pull in your line and go home for no fish is going to stay around where these creatures are. They are a type of salamander, only larger, that stays in rivers, lakes and ponds. It is a scary looking thing and if you catch one at night, the best thing to do is cut your line and let it go.

All my life I have heard about people who bragged about something that never happened. So people laughed at them and said now you will have to "face the music" or EAT CROW.

<u>Telephone Entertainment</u>

The following account of the entertainment we got from the local telephone system is a personal experience of this writer.

Two shorts and a long. That was our number. A short was one crank of the ringer. A long was two or three continuous cranks. It usually worked. If it didn't work, we tried again.

Before major telephone companies came to the Ozarks,

we established our own. It was called a party line, since only a few people were on the line. We bought a wall phone. We called it that since it hung on the wall. It was placed in a room closest to the line coming in. This saved us from running wire all over the house. A line was run around over the hills to six or eight neighbors. No telephone poles were needed. There were plenty of trees. We did need to buy a few insulators to use when we attached a wire to a tree. This kept the line from picking up too much noise.

Of course, our phone system had some disadvantages. Now and then a limb would fall on the wire and the system wouldn't work. We didn't have an operator to tell us what to do. There were no 800 numbers. A long wait wouldn't get an operator. We couldn't enjoy any classical music if we had to wait for the person we called to answer. There were no repairmen. We repaired ourselves. The FCC didn't pay any attention to us and there were no telephone bills.

One major advantage was that if we got on the line with a neighbor two or three miles away, we could stay on as long as we wanted to, unless someone else wanted to talk to another neighbor.

"Are you about ready to get off the line? You've been on there for two hours."

That was an exaggeration. We never talked that long unless we had an interesting conversation going. And we had rather good phone etiquette. We'd get off as soon as we could. But to get us off, we could hear a click click as they lifted the receiver to let us know they still wanted the line.

A second advantage was that if someone was on the line, we couldn't talk but we could listen. Often I would get my stool and listen, just listen and listen. I had to have a stool to reach the receiver.

"That preacher got pretty high and mighty last night, didn't he? I thought he was goin' to keep us all night. Musta been 12:00 o'clock when we got home. Don't seem like that helps much. Didn't help me much. Did it help you?"

"Naw, not much. I was sittin' behind Polly Ann Spivit. She wiggled on her seat all the time. But they say she's pregnant. She don't look it but Skeeter Boy Clough has been tellin' around that she is and that it is his.

"Don't believe everything you hear. Skeeter Boy would like to make us think he performed a miracle and got Polly Ann pregnant. Could be though. You never can tell what's goin' to happen around here."

"Are you goin' to the picnic Friday and Saturday nights? Think we might go Friday night."

"Yeah, we may go. But I got tired of it last year. Too many drunks. Too many fights. Too hot. Dangerous. Joe Tom says it's like hell up there. But I don't think it is that bad. Found a big black bug in my lemonade last year at Freddie Lee Johnson's stand. Told him about it. It was floatin' on top of my glass. He just skimmed it off and brought it back to me. I don't like no bugs in my lemonade."

"Bug like that wouldn't have had a chance in what some of them were drinking."

"No, might have made it drunk."

"You heard about Toe Heel Johnson bein' sick? Say he has fever every night. Gets sick at his stomach. Flounces around in the bed. Gets out of his head. Got something. He's done this for years. Seems to get worse."

"Never kept him from raisin' kids though. Been sick all his life and Sarah Jane has been pregnant about every year since they got married. How many they got now?"

"Twelve, I think."

"Proves what my grandma told me once. She said a woman should beware of a sickly man. Just stays around the house and keeps her pregnant all the time."

"Sad."

"I'd say, sad. Yes, sad."

"I keep feelin' someone is listening in on us. You feel that way?"

"Yeah, but I don't care. If it does them any good, let 'em listen."

"Your green beans comin' along good? Mine are lower than last year. Planted 'em wrong, I guess."

"Yeah, mine...."

This was when I quietly let the receiver down and got off my stool and started to do something else. I was a little afraid they did know someone was on the line. But they wouldn't ever know who it was. And that talk about green beans didn't interest me much. But I had heard some interesting talk. And since the B battery was weak in the radio and I couldn't hear *Jack Armstrong* very well, listening to all of this gave me something to do and I'll have to admit I enjoyed it.

We didn't use our phone to call the doctor or anything like that. He was not on our line. The only access we had was to the six or eight neighbors. But it was important to talk and listen to them. It was like getting the news anytime we wanted it.

If something happened that was important or exciting, we called someone on our line and soon it was known throughout the community, because they called someone else and that person called another one and on and on. It wasn't gossip. It was news. Oh, I guess sometimes it wasn't either. It was just talk but we all liked to hear it regardless of what it was.

I didn't get to use the phone much. In the first place it was too high on the wall for me so I had to get my stool to ring and my folks said I talked too much and that the neighbors wouldn't like it much if I took the line too long. But I didn't care much. I could lie on the floor and get a pretty good idea about the news by just listening to one end of the conversation and I could slip around and listen as I told you before. Sometimes Grandma would look back over her shoulder at me there on the floor and sorta indicate that she would like some privacy but she never did say anything so I just went on listening.

But once in a while I got my stool and called someone. I enjoyed cranking the longs and shorts more than I did talking.

Most of us on the line bought the same brand name of phone. Our phone was an Andrae, made somewhere in the North or East.

If someone in the community or county or somewhere thought we were interested in a phone line, a man, usually a man, would come around and tell us how much we would enjoy it and how good his phones were and what others had bought his brand. And in a few days he would come back to talk to us again. He waited just long enough for us to get together and talk about that it wouldn't cost too much for the wire and insulators and we could do the work of keepin' up the line and how nice it would be to talk to each other. So by this time everyone was ready to buy a phone.

This type of enjoyment and entertainment was popular in the 1920s, 30s and 40s. It was about the cheapest entertainment anyone ever had in the Ozarks.

<u>Dancing</u>

Many people in the Ozarks liked to dance. The most

popular dances were the waltz, two-step, square dance and the jig.

When local gatherings were popular such as the pie suppers, cake suppers, play parties, and picnics, one of the major enjoyments was the dance, usually the jig. No one knows when jig dancing, as we know it, began but people of all ages have been doing it for years. It may be one of the oldest dances of the Ozark Mountains. It is a folk dance that has been handed down generation after generation.

Some people always like to dance and everyone liked to watch. If a square dance was organized and someone did not want to join the square, there was always room on the sides of the dance floor for a jig dancer to do their thing.

The jig is an individual dance. It requires no formation, no designated steps. Everyone has his or her own free style.

However, according to people in this area, there are a few things that a jig dancer must do and not do. An elderly man in the Ozarks told me that if one wanted to be a good jig dancer, there were certain things to know.

As the dancer dances, the feet must not be more than about six inches from the floor. The jig dancer, according to most dancers, does not do high kicks but some do. They do not slap leather unless it can be done with the feet about six inches from the floor. (Slapping leather is touching the bottom of the shoes while dancing.) But regardless of what the jig dancer does, the most important thing is to keep time to the music. And the jig dancer does not do cartwheels. (Cartwheels are done by rotating one leg in a fast clockwise motion during the dance.)

Good dancers stressed that the dancer must keep time to the music. If there is a fiddle, guitar, banjo, mandolin and a bass making the music, the jig dancer may keep time to the best of any or all of them. However, many prefer to keep time to the fiddle or guitar.

Most of the action of the dancer is from the waist down. Sometimes the arms will not move much but hang down along the sides of the body. However, some upper body movement such as bringing the arms up in front of the chest, swinging the arms, clipping or making rhythmic movements of the head and shoulders may help some dancers keep better time to the music.

A jig dancer liked for the band to play a lively, fast tune. Some fiddle tunes were too slow for the dancer. People who did a lot of jig dancing liked *Mississippi Sawyer* and *Arkansas Traveler*. Also, *Orange Blossom Special* was a favorite because of the variety of speed of the tune.

The dancers would dance on anything. Often the floor was rough and the boards were uneven. But sometimes the dancers would take time before the dance to select good boards and make the surface as smooth as possible. From time to time the floor would be covered with something like meal or powder so the dancer's shoes would not stick to the floor.

Almost everyone who grew in the Ozarks could dance. But some, either from lack of opportunity or other reasons, never learned and had to be content with watching rather than dancing. Gordon McCann, an amateur folklorist and guitar player, who lives in Springfield, Missouri, told me he never had the opportunity to attend many square dances and to learn the many figures that are a part of them. He said, "When you are first learning and make a mistake, they'll laugh with you. Most dancers are very tolerant of beginners. But after awhile, if you don't improve and they start laughing at you, then you'd better learn in a hurry or forget it."

Some people did not believe in dancing. They thought it

was a sin and anyone who danced was bound for hell. This belief by some kept discontent going in some of the churches. It even caused a row now and then. And sometimes it got to the point of coming before the church meeting at which time, as we will discuss later, members were voted out of the church and told not to return.

However one man told me a simple solution to the problem. "If everybody will leave their booze at home and just come to dance and have fun, then everything will be all right. But you can make anything bad and you can make any place bad and when you do you won't have any fun and someone will get fractious and trouble will start and the next day it will be all over the community exactly what happened and them that don't like to dance will stir and stir until they make something big out of it. All this makes good people who like to dance look like heathens. The best thing to do is don't let them push you around. We never did let that happen; no we never let anybody push us around."

Weddings and Charivaris

In the Ozarks as a girl grew up she was supposed to make thirteen quilts before she got married. The THIRTEENTH was to be her wedding or bride quilt which she took with her the first night of her marriage. Quilting this many quilts was supposed to keep her mind in the right place.

The lore of superstitions had its place in wedding customs. It was unlucky for a bride to look in a mirror after she was dressed for the wedding. To marry a man whose name began with the same letter as the woman was an unlucky step. The bridegroom should not see the bride's trousseau before the wedding. And a girl should place a piece of someone's wedding cake under her pillow if she wanted to dream of her future husband.

Many weddings in the early part of the 1900s were held in the bride's home. The whole neighborhood was invited. After the wedding, a supper was served for friends and family.

If the girl happened to get pregnant before the couple planned to get married, or just got pregnant without any thought of marriage, they had a shotgun wedding. This was a hurry-up wedding and simply meant that the father of the girl would be after the boy with a shotgun if they didn't get married soon.

These shotgun weddings were not often held in the home or church but several miles away at the home of a Justice of the Peace who had the authority to marry people.

But sometimes, even if the girl was six or seven months into her pregnancy, the mother would insist that they have a home wedding with all the trimmings.

Now this got whispers from the community. "She's so brazen that she would have had that "show-off" wedding if the girl had been as big as a cow."

In most cases no one dared to ask to have a shotgun wedding in the local church. This would have caused a stink that would have split the church wide open.

One time a southern Missouri preacher went out of the community to preach a revival, and, as the gossip went, got a young girl pregnant. He was too old for her and it would have caused him a great deal of trouble so he brought the girl back home with him and married her to his younger brother who was about her age.

Some men of the community said that it didn't look like the preacher's brother would want to marry a girl who was going to have a kid by someone else.

But one man said, "Oh hell, Joe Don is so dumb about things like that. If the kid had been crawlin' around in bed the next morning after the wedding, he woulda thought it was his."

The night after the wedding was designated as the time for the charivari but sometimes the ones planning the event would wait for several days just to keep the new bride and groom wondering when to expect them.

The people giving the charivari would wait until as late as possible at night or until they thought the couple was in bed. Then they would march close to the house and begin shooting shotguns, ringing cowbells and making as much noise as possible. And they usually had good organized plans. One group would take the groom and ride him on a rail if he did not treat them and often if he did promise a treat. Sometimes they threw him in a creek or nearby pond. Another group would focus their attention on the bride. They might carry her to a nearby creek and let her "BOTTOM END" down into the cold water, bring her out, wait a few minutes, then let her down again a little deeper, all the time threatening to throw her in completely. Another group was doing their thing. They stayed at the house and put salt or meal in the couple's bed, tied cow bells to the bed springs or arranged the bed frame or bed slats so the bed would fall to the floor as soon as the couple got in bed.

The groom, if he was smart, would have candy, cookies, cigars and other treats for the hungry intruders. So after they had had their fun, they were invited into the house for the treats which they devoured savagely. Often they did not have to be invited into the house. They just came on in and did what they pleased.

Sometimes the bride's mother got excited and feared that the pond was too cold for her new son-in-law or that the ride on the rail was just too rough on him so she gave the fun makers a piece of her mind.

But there was no need to plead for mercy or get angry. The gang did what they came to do. There was no stopping them. They were going to have their entertainment.

Photography

Many liked to take pictures and they liked to have their pictures taken. From the first part of the 20th century well into the 1940s, if someone was asked if they had a camera, they might have said, "Yes, er well, I have a Kodak."

Photography was a means of entertainment that many people enjoyed. They took pictures of anything they liked or that was of great value to them or they took pictures to get attention and just have fun. They took pictures of all-day-meetin's-and-dinner-on-the-ground, of their horses, of their cars if they had one, of marriage ceremonies, of dead people, of baptisms, of their babies or anything that would give them some entertainment at the time and later as they looked at the pictures.

The picture on the right indicates that one man wanted some attention. He wanted to entertain himself and others by climbing a tree to have his picture made. In some communities not everyone could afford a Kodak. But if someone in the community had one, they were glad to lend it to a neighbor so they could have some pictures too.

Most film had to be mailed to a company that developed the pictures. This usually took from two to three weeks. So by the time they were returned people were anxiously waiting to see how they looked or if they had taken the picture correctly.

The following are a few more examples of what people were interested in when someone was around to take their picture:

The young man in the picture on the left had to have his horse shod. It was a very important event for him so he had someone to take his picture.

The picture on the right of a young man and his horse lets us know that in the early part of the century, a value was placed on a good horse and the boy was happy to have his picture made with him.

Max Decker, Ed. D.

One could say that "three men on a mule" was the setting for the picture above. No doubt, the men in the picture and the person who took it had a lot of fun

And who would not enjoy themselves in a fancy car, equipped with mud chains, in the early part of the 20th century.

Kangaroo Court

Five or six times a year people in communities in the Ozark Mountains would get together at the district schoolhouse on a Friday or Saturday night and enjoy themselves with a session of Kangaroo Court.

They would meet about dark. The women would go on into the schoolhouse and visit; the kids would run and play outside and the men would get together and decide who they were going to "try" that night. They would select a judge, lawyers for the defense and for the prosecution, a sheriff and the judge would select a jury.

Selecting the accused was the most difficult task. To keep everyone happy and avoid a row, they had to charge the person they were going to "try" with something that neither they nor their family was guilty of in real life. For example, if the one charged had an illegitimate child or any of his family had one, it would not have been wise to have made a charge related to that. Stealing chickens would have been a better charge.

The trial was carried out just like a real trial at the county seat. Often the judge would call for a recess so everyone could enjoy some cake and coffee brought by the ladies of the community.

Sometimes the court lasted until midnight or after before the jury reached a verdict.

Charges that were often made and tried were stealing chickens, cussin' your mule, watering your milk before it went to market, playing the fiddle, dancing, hunting out of season, cutting wood on another person's property, shooting another man's dog or killing someone's cat.

It was agreed before the court began that the judge selected would have complete control of the court and the courtroom at all times. And, most judges selected liked to use their power granted them by the people there.

After the trial was over and court was dismissed those attending had another piece of cake and a cup of coffee and laughed and talked about what went on during the court.

A time like this gave everyone something to talk about until something else happened in the community to direct their attention away from Kangaroo Court.

Fun with Anvils, Cotton Rocks and Shot Guns

It seemed to be good entertainment for neighbors to build a huge fire on a desolate hillside, put several anvils in the fire and listen to the loud pops of the anvils when they became hot. This was an exciting activity during the winter months, especially on Christmas day or New Years. Once in a while a man would pop an anvil when his wife gave birth to one of their children. The popping could be heard for two or three miles if the wind was just right.

Cotton rocks, large rocks that were flat and white in color, were placed in fires and gave the same effect as the anvil. People who have done this tell me that it took less heat to pop a cotton rock than it did for an anvil. Popping cotton rocks was done on the same dates as popping anvils--Christmas, New Years and on special dates for a family. Not many were popped on Independence Day since the large fire needed was dangerous at that time of the year.

There were other types of rocks that would pop under high heat but the cotton rock seemed to pop easier and louder than other rocks.

On Christmas morning and New Year's morning many people liked to let it be known that they were aware of what time of year it was so they went to the outside of the house and shot their shotgun several times. Neighbors who heard the shot answered with a shot from their guns. It was interesting to shoot several times and stop and listen for an answer.

It is said that one man in southern Missouri who had

eleven children shot his shotgun several times one morning when he found that his wife was not pregnant again. Unlike the man who popped the anvil when his wife gave birth to one of their children, this man was telling the neighborhood that they had had enough.

These three ways of producing sound to celebrate something special was an entertainment that gave them much satisfaction.

<u>Memorial Day or Decoration Day Activities</u>

People in these mountains looked forward to all holidays. But the one they seemed to enjoy and feel an obligation to attend was Memorial Day. It was an all-day affair. It was not a come-and-go event. Women cooked and took dinner. The men and children were dressed in their best. Whatever they did at the graveyard was in respect for those who had "gone to a better place".

At noon after they ate, they had a speaker, usually a preacher or a good speaking man from the county seat, who spoke about the purpose and meaning of this day. He often spoke about those who were buried there that he had known. It seemed it was easy for him to say many good things about anyone.

When he was finished, people roamed the graveyard dropping little flowers on about every grave. The flowers were not elaborate sprays from a florist. They could not afford that but what they had meant just as much, maybe more.

Some of the men of the community could not stand to see some graves without flowers on them. Baxter Gaulding, my wife's grandfather and his brother Landon Gaulding often picked large baskets of roses and took them to the graveyard and placed a rose on every grave.

Several days before Memorial Day or Decoration Day as many called it, the men had a working. They cut the grass, worked on the fence, picked up rock and did about anything that needed to be done.

They respected their dead and did everything they could to let it be known.

To Course a Bee

When people wanted some adventure and when they got hungry and couldn't get any honey from their hives, they looked to the woods. They liked the adventure and the challenge about as much as they did the honey. One man not far from Elijah, Missouri could course or "trace" a bee as he called it. He would take a good look at the sky around flowers and plants where bees might be feeding and watch a bee fly away. Then he would follow in that direction. Most of the time he would find a hollow tree full of honey that he would mark and return later with proper clothing to rob the bees of the honey. His mark on the tree let others know that he had found the tree with the honey and it belonged to him. Most everyone would honor his mark. His mark might be his first initial.

This was a form of entertainment and a source of food for the man and his family.

Chapter 11

Farm Customs

The Ozarks are essentially rural, although there are some urban areas, such as Springfield and Joplin. So farm customs are a major part of the lore. Major farm activities were enjoyed by members of the community and they looked forward to the time the event would take place. If a man planned to pick his corn on Wednesday of the next week, everyone knew about it, talked about it and wanted to know about how many bushels of corn he thought he might have. So work became a part of the recreation as neighbors swapped work and got the big jobs done at the right time. No job was too small or too big for someone to solve.

In addition to these big jobs that they liked, there were annoying things that happened that had to have attention and neighbors were there to give advice and help with them too. For example, in most communities someone had a dog that would suck eggs. And nobody wanted to lose good eggs. A man from near Mansfield, Missouri, told me about a way to stop a dog from doing such a thing. He said the best way, aside from killing the dog, was to find an Indian turnip and put it inside an egg shell. Now an Indian turnip is a wild plant that grows along the creeks in sandy soil. It has three leaves and sometimes has red or orange berries on it. Inside it has sharp growths all through it. If a person bites into one, it is like biting into a thousand needles. A suck-egg hound would remember if they bit into one. So to give a neighbor this remedy was a great help. For nothing is as bothersome as a no good suck-egg hound. Passing on this remedy was cooperation.

The work and the cooperation went on all year. In the spring there was the planting of corn. In the summer months the threshing of grain was the main activity. And during the fall and winter months the butchering, soap making, and hominy making took their time and energy.

To help with community work and your neighbor's work has been characteristic of good citizens of the Ozarks from the first settlements through the 40s and 50s. And some people remember what their parents and grandparents did for others and continue to carry on the tradition. If your neighbor helps you and you help him; if you eat at his table and he eats with you, there is a close feeling which develops that gives strength to man's relationship in a community.

It would be difficult for people in other parts of the country to understand the "help bond" that existed in the Ozark Mountains.

Even in periods of crisis the feeling that there is a man down the road or across every hollow who will give his assistance, understand one's problems, help when help is needed, and share one's sorrows gives a man or woman something that helps them stand and move on.

The "help bond" enabled the people of the Ozarks to build a life filled with contentment, love and appreciation. It gave the people an assurance that they were not alone on the mountain.

Hill people did many things in order to survive, to have

enough to eat. "Holed-up" meant that they dug a hole in the ground about two feet deep and lined it with straw. They covered whatever they put in the hole with three or four feet of dirt in the shape of a mound. There they would keep apples, potatoes and turnips all winter.

Most people like butter. If they didn't have a churn for making it, they used a quart or half gallon fruit jar. They filled the jar almost full of milk cream and shook and shook and shook and shook until the cream turned to butter.

Some people had churns that had a handle that they turned which made a paddle turn inside the churn and moved the cream even better than shaking the jar. It was probably a Daisy Churn.

Some people had a crock which held about two gallons or more that they filled with cream and stirred it with a paddle that went in an up and down motion.

One farm custom was to grow a long row of collards. People used it as a green salad. It is from the kale family. Some say it is like a cross between a cabbage and mustard.

When the men went to the field to work they wore work shoes called brogans. They were made from rawhide. They kept their Sunday shoes to wear to church and to other special events.

Farm people liked to have as much fun as anyone. One time a woman was hoeing in her garden. The hired man saw her and said, "I hope she's got on pants cause them taters have eyes."

Most hill people lived on farms and most farms had an abundance of flies. They were always bad during the summer months. Not all houses in the Ozarks had screen doors or screen over the windows so the flies would fly anywhere they wanted to.

The women were the fly-fighters because they were the

ones who cooked the food and they knew they wanted to be sanitary and they knew there was nothing as dirty as a fly.

In the 20s and 30s some people had "fly-swatters;" some had fly traps that they baited with something sweet and when the flies went in, they couldn't get out and some had enough money to go the local store and buy "Sticky Fly Paper." But some made their own paper and it worked just as well as that which they bought at the store.

Virginia Loomis Thurman who grew up south of Cabool, Missouri, found a recipe written in one of her grandfather's books published in 1903. It was a recipe for "Sticky Fly Paper." It read as follows:

"Take two pounds of rosin.
Take one pint of castor oil.
Mix together until it looks like molasses.
Don't heat it too much.
Take a small paintbrush
And spread it over fairly strong paper like wrapping paper.
This is not a bad fly catcher."

Many farm customs gave farm children a delight. They liked to go to the rural store with their parents. They were always glad if they needed to buy a gallon of coal oil, or kerosene. When the store keeper filled the can, they placed a small potato or a gumdrop on the spout of the can so the oil would not spill out. Children always wished for the gumdrop. It tasted like coal oil but they ate it anyway. It was probably good for them because it probably got rid of the worms that some children had at that time.

Farm people had a name for everything that was wrong with their livestock. My father told me that during the 30s around Tecumseh, Missouri, people had several sick cattle, especially during the winter months. Some said that their cattle had a disease they called "hollow tail." My father said it was "hollow belly" from lack of food.

A man from near West Plains, Missouri told me that in the Ozarks the weather had to be very hot, ninety degrees or more, for cocklebur to grow or for candidates for office to get excited about a farmer's vote.

Farmers always liked to have a melon patch. They said that watermelons would grow faster and bigger and have a sweeter taste if they were fertilized with a shovel full of cow manure in each hill.

Sometimes farmers had trouble with people stealing their melons. They often stopped this by selecting some of the best melons that someone would like to have and injecting croton oil with a syringe into the melon. Croton oil is a strong cathartic.

Farmers had to be on the lookout when their cattle or horses acted crazy and frothed at the mouth. They said they had been eating loco-weed which is a form of hemp.

Another caution that farm families had to take was trying to kill certain weeds or flowers in their pastures. Larkspur is a beautiful wild flower. Its color is a beautiful blue and purple. It grows in fields and along the roads in poor soil. But farmers thought it was poisonous to cattle and other animals.

A lady in Mountain View, Arkansas told me how to make a light when there was no kerosene for the lamp or lantern.

1. Cook-down the fat from possums and coons and use the grease for fuel.
2. Do not use this grease in lamps because it makes too much soot and that makes the lamp globes too black.

3. You need to make a different kind of wick. Take pieces of cloth and tie them together into a piece about four feet long. Have one person twist one end one way and another person twist the other end the other way until the string of cloth is tight.
4. Then dip it in the grease from the animal.
5. Next, hang it out in the sun to dry.
6. Then place it in a lid or flat pan. It will curl up in the lid or pan like a snake.
7. Next light the fringe of the cloth and it will give off enough to see to get around.

If rural people in the Ozarks had a dog or some other animal that began to walk as if they were blind or too sick to walk straight, they said they must have the "blind staggers." Some believed that this symptom was a sign that the dog was about to go "mad." If it was "mad", they believed it had rabies or hydrophobia. And if there was anything that people were afraid of, it was a "mad" dog. Of course this could happen to a city dog the same way but it seemed that farm families got more excited about it.

<u>Butchering</u>

Two of the most interesting events on the farm were hog-killing or butchering and when the thrasher came. Farmers wanted to kill hogs as soon as the weather got cold enough to keep the meat. So November was as soon as most people got to butcher.

The family arose early on the day set for killing hogs. While the father did the chores and the mother cooked the breakfast, the children would go to the pond and break ice for they would need plenty of pond water during the day. Next the children would gather limbs, cobs, chunks of wood and stumps and build a fire under the large kettle. By the time they had finished building the fire, everyone went to the house for breakfast.

While the water was heating they would eat and wait for the neighbor who had promised to help them. After the neighbor arrived and the water was hot, the men went to the pen and shot the hog between the eyes and stuck a sharp knife in its throat so it would bleed good. Before the hog was dragged to a platform on which it would be scalded and scraped, the men cut a gambling stick which was used to hang the good fat hog. This was a stick about two feet long sharpened on both ends. Each end was forced between the leg muscles of the rear legs of the hog. The hog was then drug to a platform that was about one foot high. At one end of the platform was a large barrel filled with hot water from the kettle.

Even though the hog might weigh four hundred pounds, the men put it into the barrel which was set at an angle. They would pull it in and out, in and out. They were very careful to turn the hog often because they did not want the hair to set. After the hair began to slip, the hog was pulled out of the barrel and everyone went to work with sharp knives and scraped the hog clean.

As soon as this task was finished, the hog was swung by lifting it and placing the gambling stick over a pole which had been chained to a nearby tree. Now they were ready to gut the hog. Soon the women came to take the fat from the guts. Nothing was wasted. Next the hog was placed back on the platform which had been cleaned of the hair, to be cut into desired pieces. A chopping ax and a saw were used for this.

If the men had any luck with scalding, they would have three or four hogs killed and cut up by dinner time. So a side of ribs and a string of tenderloin was cut from the hog and sent to the house to be cooked.

After dinner the men sat around and talked about the task they had just completed.

When the neighbors left they were given a good mess of meat. I always thought my mother was just a little too generous. She sent half the ribs and it seemed like half the tenderloin. I always thought she should have sent more liver.

Later in the afternoon the meat was taken to the smokehouse and covered with plenty of salt. In a few weeks it would be hung and hickory smoked.

Threshing

During the long hot days of July and August, the big thrasher always made its rounds through the community. Although the owner of the thrasher brought his own crew, several men followed along looking for extra work. And of course the neighbors came and spent the entire day at the farmer's place.

The noon meal was the major attraction to everyone with the thrashing crew. Harvest hands were always looking for a table full of food so a dinner "fit for a thrasher" was cooked. One man tells of a thrasher hand who ate so much he made himself sick. It is said that he ate twenty-four biscuits, twelve pieces of fried chicken, one-half gallon of milk, two bowls of cobbler and several servings of fruits and vegetables. For sure, no one went back to the field hungry for the ladies of the neighborhood had all brought food and helped the lady of the house cook during the morning.

When the thrashing was finished, the owner and all the men moved on to the next farm where the neighbors had again come to work and cook.

The straw stack left by the thrasher always made a nice place for the children to play. And when it was not eaten by cattle, it provided a good place for a watermelon patch the following summer.

Many times the people who ran the thrasher stayed all night with the farmer. They would work until about dark and come in and eat a big supper. After supper they either talked, told stories or played musical instruments and sang. Many workers always brought their fiddle and banjo along. Sometimes they would sing and play until midnight but they were always up at 6:00 o'clock for breakfast and another day with the thrasher.

One day a traveling salesman from a large city came by about time for breakfast. He talked for awhile and told the farmers where he was going and what he was trying to sell. The farmers seemed to like him so they asked him to stay for dinner.

"Oh, that would be too long," the salesman said.

"Only until about twelve. The ladies are not often late with dinner they know we are hungry about that time so they are pretty much on time with dinner," said Josh Blakemore.

"Well where I come from they call that meal you eat about noon lunch. Then they call the meal at the end of the day dinner," the salesman replied.

"We don't care what you call what you eat. We ain't going to worry about that. If you want to eat our dinner for lunch or our supper for lunch or our lunch for dinner, you are welcome to eat. But don't get everything complicated. We've got wheat to thrash and when we get tired and hungry, were goin' to eat no matter what you or anyone calls it. So you are welcome to stay and eat. Eat all you want. We don't want anyone to go away from our place under-fed. We want them to know that we are neighborly so do what you want to," Uncle Josh said, as he threw the harness on a mule.

Molasses Making

Making molasses was an annual event in each community. Everyone looked forward to the time when the "molasses maker" would start his work.

The power that was used to squeeze the juice from the cane was a horse fastened to a long pole which acted as a lever. As the horse was driven around and around, two steel rollers pressed the cane. The cane was forced between the rollers by hand and the juice ran out into a barrel. The molasses was made near a spring so they would have plenty of water. The molasses pan was set on a furnace about three feet from the ground. As the fire burned under the pan, the cane juice was kept moving by partitions which were made in the pan. This let the juice go from one end of the pan to the other when the maker thought it was ready. As the juice cooked, it was very important that it be skimmed often. As the fire kept getting hotter and hotter and as the skimming continued, the juice began to thicken. When it got to a certain thickness, it was sampled by the expert, the "molasses maker." If he thought it was the correct thickness, had the correct taste and was not dark, it was run out of the pan into a barrel. It was usually strained as it ran into the barrel.

Many molasses makers have been accused of straining the juice through their sock and some have been seen spitting tobacco juice in the pan. But that was probably not true and it didn't make any difference to someone who wanted to eat some molasses. Ozark molasses was good and made some of the best molasses cookies in the world.

Chapter 12

Church Activities

The local church was a major center of community activity. It was here and at the district school that all the important gatherings took place. It was at the country church that people in the Ozarks taught their children some of the best "God fearing and God loving religion. They sang "When the Roll is Called up Yonder," "Oh Why Not Tonight" among other songs. They shook the hands of their brothers as tears streamed down their cheeks. They got on their knees at the altar and prayed to God on high. Their hearts became tender; their thoughts became holy; their spirits were revived by love for God and for their brother. The Ozarker was a man of God.

Yet there were those among them that could cause more hell and more ill feeling than anyone could imagine. This type of person was in the minority, but they made themselves known to everyone as they told lies, ran around with "wild" women, cursed the ways of the Lord and drank their liquor. But they made their way to most churches and services and perched themselves in every "amen" corner of every church in the community.

The major functions of the church will be discussed in All-Day-Meetings and Dinner-on-the-Ground, Church Meetings, Church Debates, Baptizings, Protracted

Meetings, The Brush Arbor and How People took care of the Preacher.

These church functions were not only a part of the church program for the year but also a type of entertainment for all.

All-Day-Meeting and Dinner-on-the-Ground

I am proud to say that I have had the experience of attending "all-day-meetings and dinner-on-the-ground." Such an occasion was held two or three times a year.

When the preacher announced that come next Sunday there would be preachin' in the morning, dinner on the ground at noon and singing in the afternoon, the members of the church became excited and planned and talked about it during the entire week.

They could have called it "dinner outside" because the food was not put on the ground. The men of the church would build long tables out of rough boards or they would bring out the long seats from the church house and put them together. This way one sorta looked down on the food. Sometimes these benches stretched for forty or fifty feet because the ladies of the church seemed to think it was a sin to let someone bring more than they did.

I will never forget the delicious food that the ladies of the church would prepare. There would be gooseberry cobbler, blackberry cobbler, chicken and dumplings, pickles, beets, onions, brown beans with large hunks of sowbelly, fried chicken, flour gravy, chicken gravy, red-eye or raised gravy, ham gravy, sweet potatoes, pies, cakes, young squirrel and rabbit, ham meat and side pork.

But for some reason the most wonderful treat of all was when someone brought "store boughten' light bread. It wasn't as good as biscuits or cornbread. But it had a different smell and we didn't have it very often so I guess it was good because it was different.

Just about everyone brought their dinner to set with the others, but now and then someone would come to eat without bringing a single thing. Of course they were allowed to eat but the talk among the ladies after dinner was, ". . . if they can afford to run all over the country to sales and parties, they could afford to bring dinner now and then."

Another thing that seemed to worry some of the women were the flies that invaded the food when it was put out on the benches. Two or three of them would station themselves along the benches of food and swing away at any fly they could see and they could see plenty of them. They knew that they were nasty. But other women just let them fly and crawl all over the food as if they were a part of the event.

The picture below is a picture of an "all-day-meeting and dinner-on-the-ground somewhere in southern Missouri in the 1930s. The women were putting out the food, the kids were in the way, and the men were just

standing there ready for a wonderful meal.

It seems that this type of church event always came in the summer time when it was hot, very hot. It was too hot to leave food out in the open very long or it would spoil. It was so hot as they ate that someone suggested to the preacher that summer dinners should be discontinued. And it was hot inside as they began the afternoon of singing. Most everyone came in except for a few who wanted a longer smoke or chew after the great meal so they hung around the front door or looked in the windows to see what was going on.

After dinner was over, and while the women were putting the leftovers in a big cardboard box, the men relaxed against a big rock or tree or went down over the hill to the "open air" toilet or talked about the morning sermon or gossiped about someone. Soon they all went inside and sang all afternoon.

The preacher got up first and had prayer and then he introduced the man who would have charge of the singing. In fact he would lead the singing, except for the quartets and solos. So the man in charge took over. He asked that everyone stand on the first song. That was a good idea because it already was like an oven in the church house.

Brother John Houts was seated with his wife and mother-in-law about three rows up from the back. They were singing and enjoying themselves but were extremely hot. Brother John wiped sweat with his red handkerchief while his wife and mother-in-law and about everybody else fanned with a cardboard of some kind. Not many had fans with a handle.

Right in front of Brother John and his family was Sister Lou Ellen Maples and her three girls. Sister Lou Ellen was a big woman and rather fat. She had on a thin dress but she was hot. Sweat ran down her neck. The louder she sang and the more she fanned with the cardboard the hotter she got, it seemed.

Singing had gone for about an hour when the leader suggested again that they all stand and get a little comfort from the heat, maybe. So they did stand, but continued singing.

About this time Brother John looked down and saw that Lou Ellen's dress had caught in the center of the two fleshy parts of her buttocks. So without thought and being the kind man that he was he reached down and gently pulled the dress out from where it was caught.

Now Sister Lou Ellen was known for her quick temper and fast reactions without stopping to think much about them. So seeing and feeling what someone from behind was doing, she whirled around and as some of the men would have said, "if it hadn't been in church, slapped the hell out of Brother John."

Well, John was taken aback as everyone heard the loud slap and looked around. Brother John's face got green, red and all colors but he continued looking at his songbook and singing along. He took out his red handkerchief, wiped sweat again and looked at his wife and mother-in-law who were looking down. He didn't know what to do. He knew he had made a grave mistake by trying to be helpful, but not thinking how the sister would react. So, in his confused predicament, without thinking again but trying to make things right, he gently took his trigger finger and pushed the dress back into the place from which he had pulled it out. Well this caused more problems. Lou Ellen turned around with hesitation and slapped him again. Everyone looked back and around at poor brother John but kept on singing *Throw Out the Lifeline*.

It wasn't long before Brother John's wife nudged him and they left the church house. No one stopped singing and sister Lou Ellen kept on sweating and fanning and she looked around now and then to the empty seats behind her.

Now this story of the unlucky brother and slappin' sister is told and gossiped about from the time it happened forty or fifty years ago to the present. I can't say for sure that it is true because I was outside with the other boys and several men when all this took place. But I have a good idea that it was.

Church Business Meetings

Fifty or sixty years ago the church meetin' was just about an annual affair in the Ozark Mountains. When the preacher and some of the more religious brothers of the church decided that another brother had been sinning and acting contrary to the laws of God and the church, or in other words had "back slidden," they called the members of the church together for the purpose of telling the accused brother, in public, of the charges against him. The brother was given the right to defend himself but that was about all he got to say. After he had his short say, the members present voted to retain him as a brother or "kick him out" of the church.

One of these meetings was at a schoolhouse which was being used as a church part of the time in Ozark County, Missouri; it proved to be the most colorful and dramatic one in the area. Several brothers were charged for numerous offenses.

L.S. Blane was charged for playin' a fiddle at a dance.

"What have you got to say for yourself, young man," yelled the preacher.

"I'm guilty," said Brother Blane.

"You have heard the evidence and the confession," said the preacher.

"All in favor of removing Brother Blane from the church and his name from the church book let it be known by raising your right hand."

Twenty-five hands went up.

"Those opposed, likewise," shouted the preacher.

Three hands went up. They were the hands of Brother Blane, his wife and his mother.

"You are out," whipped the preacher, as he turned to the other sinful brothers.

Others were then brought before the church. Clev Hunt was charged for cussin' his mule. He denied ever doing anything like that and pointed out that no one could have heard him if he had cause no one was around. But the vote went twenty-six to two. Brother Hunt and his wife voted against his removal.

Since no one actually heard him cussin' his mule, it was decided not to kick him out but to give him a lighter sentence. He was forbidden to read from the Bible at church and he could not sing along with the others at any time.

So the next Sunday brother Hunt came to church but before it started he boldly marched to the front of the building and wrote on the blackboard in big letters, NO READ, NO SING!

And there was Harry Bruner who was charged with drinking. He argued that it was for the bad cold he had had for weeks. But that was a poor excuse. He was put out. Peter Grant was put out for saying a wicked word about sister Luallen and Ellen Jo Wisp was found to be a disgrace in the eyes of the Lord for wearing short hair.

Some of the members took the side of the sinners. Some stayed with the preacher and the elders and deacons of the church. Despite the way they voted they later took sides and talked about it. So a meeting of this kind did two things: (1) It got rid of the brothers and sisters who had sinned in the eyes of others, and (2) sometimes caused so much ill feeling that half of the members quit, started another church and would not speak to one another for months, even years.

The Church Debate

Many Ozarkians can remember when many of the churches would hold debates. Members of the church seemed to enjoy this type of activity. Some preachers even made their living by going through the country asking others to debate them on certain issues about the word of God.

My father told me about the following debate which happened in Ozark County, Missouri sometime during the 30s.

On one occasion in the Ozark Mountains of southwest Missouri preacher Jim and preacher George were debating and several words, uncommon in religious circles, were used. It seemed while preacher George was before the church giving his views on the subject, preacher Jim spent the time winking at his rival debater. Some of the people present believed he was doing this to confuse the other man. However, it was not long until this could be taken no longer by the preacher on the floor and he threw what religion he might have had out the window and got the winker told.

"Wink and blink, you son-of-a-bitch," he said.

Well, preacher Jim stopped his winking but when his

turn came to take the floor he made mention of and explained why he was winking.

"It seems that my winking bothered our dear brother. Why God winked at ignorance, so why shouldn't I?"

This was typical of the local debate. It was said that at times preachers had to be parted and some have said they left the church with bloody noses.

But it is said that a community could create more interest, get more people in the Lord's house and create more fun and entertainment by having a church debate than any other way. People from far and near would come to hear a debate if they knew about it. Some preacher-debaters had their own following which acted like their cheering crowd.

Baptizings

Everyone went to baptizings, it seemed, whether they belonged to the church or not. This even was usually held at the end of the revival meeting and on many occasions as many as thirty or forty were baptized.

Each church had its favorite water hole for this purpose and would not change unless the members voted to do so.

On Sunday the preacher would announce that there would be a baptizing after services the next Sunday at the regular place. Members were asked to spread the word around the community.

On the next page is a picture of a baptizing in the North Fork of White River somewhere near the Missouri-Arkansas Line in the early 1900s. The weather did not bother if someone wanted to be baptized. A lady near Elijah, Missouri, told me that she had seen people baptized in the river on cold winter days when ice would cover their clothing when they came out. She believed that God took care of the exposure

to the cold for she had never known a person to get sick from the exposure.

On the day of the baptizing at about two o'clock the bank of the river would be lined with friends and relatives and other people who just wanted to come. As those who were to be baptized marched hand in hand into the clear blue mountain water, the congregation sang loud and strong. They sang *Trust and Obey*, *Where He Leads Me*, *O Happy Day*, and *Shall We Gather at the River*, among others.

Their voices carried over the water and up the hollows and into the hills from where they echoed softly back. It seemed to be a religious custom to stop singing when each person was placed under the water but when they arose, the sweet sounds of the music began again. It began with more melody, more force because their hearts had been made glad.

In the meantime, young boys who had escaped the eyes

of their mothers ran up and down the creek splashing in the water with their rocks and sticks. But no one seemed to mind. They were at their business.

When all persons had been baptized, they walked out of the water, hand in hand, as the singing continued. Joyous handshaking followed. And tears ran down their cheeks.

Perhaps this was far from the customs of an urban church; perhaps someone would say that this was an example of the "backwoods" in the Ozarks but there on that rocky shore of the river existed a reverence that no one could take away. There was a warmth for one another. There was an atmosphere that must have been pleasing to God.

Members of the church became excited when anyone was saved and baptized. They were especially happy when an elderly person for whom they had prayed for years made this giant step. They clapped their hands. They praised God. They prayed. They welcomed the person with "open arms". They were happy. They could feel God in their presence.

But someone always had a story to tell about the baptizing. Someone said that a woman wanted to be baptized in the river. So the preacher put her under. When she came up, she said, "Hell, that's cold." So the preacher had to put her under again.

Protracted Meetings

A protracted meeting was one that lasted for a week, maybe two or three. People came from far and near and stayed for several days. They slept in their wagons and cars if they had one or some had tents. Preaching went on all day long and well into the night. Some of the best preachers of the area were there. One preacher that about everyone liked was preaching one night when a dark rain cloud came up in the southwest. It looked like the people in that direction were getting a good rain. It was hot and dry at this place so the preacher stopped his sermon and pointed toward the cloud. "It is said that it rains on the just and the unjust. But you could take a gallon and water the just". Such a statement would have made some people there mad but this preacher could get by with it because he was respected for his ability to preach and for being a good man. After saying this he chuckled and went on with his sermon.

These events were usually held in the summer when it was hot and stormy. But they didn't seem to mind. They seemed to enjoy every minute of it and looked forward to it from year to year.

These events were, no doubt, a stabilizing force in the community. Not everyone attended the meetings but even those who did not agreed that they were necessary for the churches to have and gave their blessings.

The Brush Arbor

During the hot summer months many Ozark communities built brush arbors for their revivals. They were especially handy for protracted meetings which went on for weeks. They were made like a house except there were no sides and the roof was just limbs and branches of trees thrown together. Large crowds attended for it was pleasant to get out of a hot house and listen to a good sermon.

Most everyone went inside where seats had been made of long boards placed on nail kegs. However, the young boys stood outside and made for the woods as soon as the singing began. They played "Hide and Seek" and "Fox and Geese" while the singing and preaching continued. Also, a few of the men stayed outside and leaned against trees and chewed their tobacco or smoked as they did at all meetings. Their reasons for not going inside were that they just liked the fresh air, or that they didn't want to associate with some of the people who claimed to be Christians and were no better than the sinners.

The preacher was a strong voiced individual who waved his arms and shouted so much that he was drenched with perspiration by the time his sermon was over. He usually preached for about two hours and sometimes on Sundays he went for three or four. His subject, at most meetings, was about the sinners who had corrupted the world.

At times he would point his finger at those men standing outside by the trees and accuse them of having no backbone or love for anyone but themselves and that they were going to hell if they didn't change their ways. This did not bother the men. They just stood there and chewed their tobacco or rolled their own cigarettes and developed a greater dislike for that "no good" preacher.

Even if some of the members of the community didn't respond to the pleas of the preacher, there was generated among many of the people a genuine feeling of love for man and God as they met there in the wilderness in the arbor and looked to God for their goodness.

The brush arbor was also used each year for the Association meeting. One denomination always held a summer get-together. Leaders of the different churches of that faith and their preachers met for several days and sang and preached. People of that church did not say we are going to a certain town or near a place for a meeting. They said we are going to the Association and everyone knew what they meant. They went and camped out and slept in their wagons and had a good time.

So, the brush arbor was used for many things. It wasn't comfortable in the hot summer months but it was much better than having to sit in a church house and endure the heat without any ventilation.

Protracted meetings, association meetings, singings and prayer meetings were a part of the customs and culture of the people.

Chapter 13

A Death in the Family

The information about the death and burial of a person in the Ozarks is from experiences I had as a small boy. About anytime a neighbor died, I went with my parents to the neighbor's house, and watched the carpenter make the coffin and the box. I ate dinner with the family and the neighbors. I always felt sorry for the family who had lost someone. I wanted to cry sometimes.

I was eleven when my grandmother died at our house. I slipped into the room where the person who was acting like an undertaker was washing the body, combing her hair and getting her "all fixed up" the best he could. No one knew I was there but I saw everything he did. All this made me sad because Grandma had lived with us all my life.

During the time when morticians and funeral homes were almost unheard of, Ozark people cared for their dead the best they could in their own way. Although their methods were simple and crude to some people, they meant good with what they had to use.

"It's the best my pa ever had on earth," one man said as he watched his father being lowered into the grave. Large tears streamed down his cheeks but one could detect the satisfaction that was in his eyes for he thought his father was getting a nice burial.

2 Soon 2 Be 4 Gotten

When a person died, the neighbors came in to do anything they could to help. In most communities there was a man who acted as the undertaker. The first thing he did was to place quarters on the dead person's eyes after he closed them. It was important to do this as soon as possible so they would be sure to close well. The corpse was given a bath from water in large pans or from rubbing alcohol if they could afford it, a shave and a haircut if it was a man or the hair of a woman was combed the best it could be.

The community carpenter was notified and came to make the coffin and the box for the coffin. He usually set up two saw horses in the front yard of the person's home and hammered and sawed as friends talked under the trees. Pine boards were used because the carpenter could work with pine easier and faster. Covering for the inside and outside of the casket was usually bought at the local store which carried a special type of gray cloth for this purpose.

Sometimes it was difficult for some families to find money for the boards and the covering for the casket but the store owner never failed to carry them until they could pay. Sometimes he collected and sometimes he didn't.

After the bath, haircut or combing, the person was dressed. Then they were "laid out" on wide boards which rested on two saw horses. They were kept this way until the casket was finished.

On one Ozark farm, the man who had died had three grown boys. It seemed that the men who were working on the body and helping the "undertaker" could not find any boards wide enough for the "laying out" purpose. So the men went to the front yard and asked one of the boys if they had any boards of that type. The boy yelled loudly to the other brothers who were at the barn at that time.

"Hey, oh hey, Harnie. Are ye down thar at the barn? Iffin you are, look around and see iffin you can find some boards to lay Pa out on."

As soon as the casket and the box were finished, the body was placed in it and it was set in one corner of the living room of the house. After the neighbors had gone home and had done their chores, they came back and took turns staying with the body all night. A light was kept burning, also. The dim light, the stillness, the gray casket and the small bouquet of roses which had been placed on the casket gave the room a melancholy atmosphere to those who were there with the body.

Many of the neighbors brought food the next day and they stayed for at least two meals so they could help eat it.

The next day just after noon the casket was loaded on a wagon or old flat bed truck and the long journey to the graveyard began. Usually it was not far but it seemed like miles to everyone. This was a heartbreaking sight. But sometimes it was worse. It was worse if the Daddy or Mother were younger. The rattle of the wagon, the poorly dressed family, the broken hearted little boy or girl who was going on their last trip with Daddy, the pallbearers who were dressed in their new overalls all marched down the lonely road. For the old man or young man who looked on, this was not right, not good; yet there it was.

At the graveyard on a little knoll the casket was set under a large oak tree and everyone gathered around. The preacher read a long passage from the Bible and a long obituary. He then preached a revival sermon (except for calling for joiners) for about two hours. He made almost everyone cry but sent the deceased to a wonderful Heaven. He finally turned the services over to the congregation who sang *The Old Rugged Cross, When the Roll is Called up Yonder,*

Amazing Grace, and *Precious Memories,* among others.

Soon the casket was carried to the grave which had been dug that morning with pick and shovel. It was started and finished that morning because it was considered a bad omen to dig part of a grave one day and part the next. No one ever did that. As four men with leather plow lines let the big box down slowly, the family watched and cried. No son or daughter, wife or husband ever left the grave until the last shovel of dirt was thrown on the grave. To leave before this time was considered bad, ugly, and disrespectful and it was just not done.

So this was the way Uncle Joe was put to rest and the people said he had been given a good funeral. Everyone, including the family, was pleased that everything had gone as it had. On a sandstone rock which was placed at the head of his grave these words were cut--MAY HE REST IN PEACE.

As I mentioned before someone in the community acted as the undertaker when someone died. But when funeral homes came to the Ozarks, they brought with them something every woman liked. Prized possessions of women were fans with handles. Few people had any type of fan like this. They had to use a paper or a cardboard with no handle. The funeral home advertised on one side of the fan. On the other side was a pretty picture of some kind. If one wanted to get into trouble in a hurry, they could just bother or move their mother's or grandmother's fan with the wooden handle.

*Possum Trot School
near McClurg and Brownbranch
in Taney County, Missouri*

Chapter 14

One-room Schools in the Ozarks

One-room schools did several things for the Ozarks—they provided an education for children, grades one through eight; they acted as the center of community activities; and they provided jobs for teachers which were needed during the Depression.

My information about the one-room schools in the Ozarks Mountains comes from personal experience. I attended one for eight years and I taught in one for four years. The following information is important to know if one is to gain an understanding of the customs and lore created by this type of institution.

Children walked several miles to school but they didn't mind the rain, the snow, the wind or the hail. They just got ready and went without much, if any, grumbling. They usually followed the roads but it was not uncommon for some to make trails in the woods and over the mountains. Some set their rabbit traps along paths that led toward the school. This way they could check them every morning before they went on to school.

Just like today, there were good teachers and poor ones. During the 1930s it was told that some teachers got their jobs by "buying" the school. And some teachers moved around a lot from one school to another. They were usually such a poor teacher who couldn't teach anything or the older kids ran them off.

My wife, Mona Gaulding Decker, told me that it was the talk among rural school teachers of Douglas and Ozark Counties almost every year about a teacher being such a poor teacher that the county superintendent of schools in each county had a little fun out of it. When this teacher got a job teaching in one county, the superintendent of the other county would send the superintendent a sympathy card. If the same teacher crossed the county line the next year, the superintendent who lost her sent a sympathy card to the county superintendent where she moved.

Children didn't drop out much. That was not a problem. Many were over twenty years old and in the eighth grade. Sometimes the teacher would be only a few years older than the oldest student. Someone said that one little boy was held back in the second grade because they didn't want him to get ahead of his daddy in school.

Older boys would often make it rough on a teacher, especially a woman teacher and, worse yet, a young woman not many years older than they were. The boys were probably trying to get the attention from the young lady teacher. But many of these women teachers were spunky and would cut them a stick and as one board member told me, "They would just beat the hell out of some of them mean kids that needed it."

Most teachers were "tough" and didn't put up with any nonsense. They let the children have time to play but they expected them to work. Frank McClendon, mayor of Gainesville, Missouri, told me that a well known teacher during the 20s, Professor James Small of Ozark county, had the following philosophy: "Ram it in. Jam it in. Cram it in. Kids heads are hollow."

No one ever mentioned the word "basics" but they were taught anyhow. Children read, memorized poems, wrote stories, memorized the multiplication tables, memorized the principal parts of verbs, memorized the names of the Presidents, the states and their capitols, the major rivers, mountain ranges and lakes of the world. They knew how to do long division, fractions, add, subtract, multiply and divide by the time they were in the fourth or fifth grade and earlier.

By the fifth grade or earlier everyone knew what a topic sentence was, only they didn't call it that. They knew that one sentence must lead to the next and that all sentences in a paragraph must be about the same thing but they had no names for all of this. They just did it and did a good job.

Children were taught how to count money and make change. The only problem in the 30s and 40s was finding the coins to count. Most kids who went to the store and gave the merchant fifty cents for twelve cents worth of candy could count up from twelve to fifty and tell one in a few seconds how much money they were to get back.

There were no free or hot lunches. Students took their lunch in a lunch box or lunch bucket if they were lucky enough to have one but most everyone used a gallon lard bucket. Everyone looked forward to recess and lunch hour when they could eat. They knew what was in their lunch bucket for most of them had watched their mother prepare it. They would have ham between biscuits, a jar of butter and molasses, fried potatoes, tater fritters[8], cake and pie. They all ate together and knew what others had to eat. If someone saw something they liked, they might trade a tater fritter for an oatmeal cookie.

Many excellent learning experiences took place at the one-room school. Social interaction and "mentoring" went on all year. Older students helped younger ones. There was teamwork and younger students had respect for the older ones help. It seemed like every older girl adopted a younger one to care for. The concept of "hands-on" learning is not a new thing. It began years ago in the one-room school. Teachers used what they had at hand and students, for example, took sticks, pebbles, or marbles to show values of numbers in their hands and addition and subtraction became easier. While the teacher was working with fourth graders, for example, the eighth graders might be helping fifth graders with their lesson in fractions or the sixth graders might be helping the first graders with their reading assignments.

The outdoor toilets didn't have BOYS or GIRLS written on them anywhere but everyone knew where to go and where not to go. Before the time of the outdoor toilets students just went into the woods. Boys went one way. Girls went another.

For many years children drank water from one dipper. But progress took over and the teacher told everyone that they must buy a drinking cup of their own. Most of them had handles so the teacher had the students cut large numbers from calendars and paste them on the wall in a certain section close to the water bucket. Then they drove a nail underneath each number to hang their cup. Students were then assigned a number that they would have as long as they attended that school. At the end of the year the teacher told the students to take their cups home and wash them.

Along the front of the room was a chalkboard, properly called a blackboard, the teacher's desk in the center and a long bench called the recitation bench where students came before the teacher to talk about their lessons.

The ABCs were in printed and cursive letters. Students began with the printed letters and advanced to the cursive.

By using the cursive writing when they were ready for it, sometimes at an early age, many students became excellent writers.

There was a proper way for the students to go to the recitation bench. When it came time for Eighth Grade English, the teacher would say, "Eighth Grade English, rise." The students would stand by their desks. Then, the teacher would say, "Pass." At that time the students would walk quietly and take their place on the recitation bench in front of the teacher. Discussion of English would then begin.

Somewhere on the wall behind the teacher's desk were a few maps. But there was a problem with the map placement in most rural schools. The schoolhouse front door usually faced the north. So when children went in the front door, they found their seats facing south and the teacher's desk, recitation bench, blackboard and the few maps on the south wall. Since the top of the map was north, its position on the south wall made west on the left side and east on the right side. This "imprinting" may have caused students to think of California, for example, to be east and the eastern states to be thought of as being west.

About the only pictures that decorated the walls was a picture of George Washington and one of Abraham Lincoln.

Children were taught to take good care of the flag. Two students were selected each week to put the flag out on the flag pole in the mornings before the bell rang for school to begin. After the flag was on the pole, students faced the flag, placed their right hand over their heart and said the Pledge of Allegiance. The two children who put the flag on the pole each morning were responsible for watching the weather because the flag was not left out if there was any type of falling weather. At the end of the day just before school was out, the teacher let two other students, who had been selected for the same week to bring the flag in, go get the flag off the pole, bring it in and fold it. This was to be done without the flag touching the ground or the floor.

During the morning after saying the Pledge of Allegiance, they sang the National Anthem. The students always enjoyed this part of the school day.

About once a year the County Superintendent from the county seat came for a one or two hour visit. They were elected by the people so this was a good time to have some fun with the kids and make them like them so they would go home and say that the good, smart County Superintendent had been to their school. The Superintendent would say something good about the teacher and make her feel good so she and most of the parents of the kids would vote for the Superintendent at the next election.

The Superintendent always allowed time to make a little talk and tell a good story. One time he came to a school in southern Missouri and during his talk he wrote something on the blackboard. He wrote NOSMOKING. He let us look at this for awhile and then said that some poor kids somewhere didn't know how to read so they pronounced it NOSMO KING. The students liked that.

Once or twice a year during the depression someone sent things to the County Superintendent who sent them on to the teacher to give to the kids. Sometimes it was fruit. One time we got some apples and tangerines. We didn't know what the tangerines were. We thought they were dried-up oranges but we ate them and liked them. They were the first part of FDR'S handouts.

Max Decker, Ed. D.

Sometimes strange ladies, strange to the children because they didn't know them, came by school and brought little dolls, books, pencil boxes and other things that were handy and funny. They were missionary ladies who visited all the schools in the county and told Bible stories using a flannel board. Sometimes an organization called Save the Children's Federation sent things to us.

We loved these presents. It was like Christmas in the hot summer. But my folks didn't like for me to receive books and things to eat because they said it was "relief" and we were not going to take any "relief" of any kind. If we couldn't afford it, we would do without it. Some of us kids didn't much agree with that at that time but that was how it was.

And sometimes someone would come to the schoolhouse just after the noon hour and park outside. There would be bright writing on the truck and different colored stripes and pictures of cowboys and horses and girls. They were there to show a moving picture that night and they came before school was out so the students would all see the truck and go home and put up a fuss to go back that night to the show.

One time at the Colvin School in Ozark County, Missouri, they did this and several of us went that night. It was going to cost twenty-five cents to see someone called Tom Mix, I think. But about a half-hour before it was supposed to start, the man who ran the show got up and said he couldn't show it for the price that people could pay. There was not enough there. This show man probably did this trick everywhere he went to get more money, but it worked. Several of the men got together and made up a little more money to satisfy him and he went on with the show. It was exciting. Several bad people got killed and there were several men who were the best shots we had ever witnessed. The movie had one man who was good and one who was bad but both had the best horses that any of us had ever seen. But good always won out over evil. We liked the movies and played the characters at recess for months.

During the first half of the 20th century and especially during the Depression people of the school district didn't see too much need for play equipment. So what we had we made. Imagination was in full play.

We used a limb or a piece of a board for a ball bat and wrapped string for a ball. If someone had a little rubber ball, we were in luck because it could be wrapped with strings and the rubber ball would become the core of the ball and it would bounce a little and go a little more when we hit it.

We jumped the rope a lot too. We took turns bringing a piece of rope from home. Our parents didn't like this too much but we didn't hurt the ropes so most of them let us have them. Two kids turned the rope and one would jump. If you were good, you could "run in" and start jumping while they were turning the rope. Some kids got so good that they could jump over a hundred times and not touch the rope. Once in a while we got daring and wanted to "show off" a little so we asked the two students turning the rope to give us "hot pepper" which meant that they would turn the rope as fast as they could.

We had a lot of fun on "teeter totters" too. They were built by placing an old board over a big log, a stump or a rock. Then one of us would get on one end and one on the other and up and down we would go as long as we wanted.

In the fall we cleaned the leaves off the school yard. We

made a big pile and jumped in over our heads. The leaves were usually oak leaves and we would bury older students with just their heads sticking out.

Most of us played "cowboys and Indians" a lot. We used sticks for guns and if someone said, "Bang, Lee Roy," Lee Roy was dead.

Most students went barefooted as long as they could. School usually started on the second Monday in July just about the time tree frogs began to sing at full speed, so we went barefooted from then until the middle of October or until it was too cold. And no one wore shorts in the summer. We didn't know what they were and we needed some protection for our legs because no one knew when they might be chased into a briar patch or fall down on a big rock or slide ten feet in sharp gravel. So boys were overalls and girls wore dresses. Most boys were hard on shoes and when the sole would come loose at the front end of the shoe and flapped and flapped as we walked, something had to be done. So fathers took hog ringers and fastened the sole back together and it would last for awhile. And we didn't have any raincoats or overshoes. We wrapped "toesacks"[8] around our shoes and tied them with binder twine to keep out the snow and some of the rain.

The schoolhouse took a lot of abuse on Halloween. Someone always soaped the windows, turned the outhouses over if they could or put a skunk under the schoolhouse or in it. Pranksters were always dragging big logs across the road that led to the schoolhouse. They had to be moved before a wagon or car could get in.

Christmas was the big event of the year at the one-room school in the Ozarks. Preparation for Christmas began just after Thanksgiving. On a Friday afternoon the teacher took all the kids and went into the fields and woods to look for a

Christmas tree. They always got a cedar that looked small in the woods but when they put it up in the corner of the schoolhouse, it was too big and someone had to cut the bottom off so it would fit. The students brought decorations from home and made some at school during recess. They used crepe paper strips wrapped and twirled with different colors. They made paper chains from construction paper and if they were lucky the teacher might have a paper bell that folded out. They put the paper bell in the center of the room and made streamers of bright colors and attached them to the corners of the room and ran them to the bell. Sometimes they made icicles and placed them on the paper streamers.

Each child would color Christmas pictures and make scenes to hang on the windows. At this time children could be seen tracing pictures pressed against the windows for more light to make a pattern. If it was needed one child would hold the paper for another so the page wouldn't tear and they would get a good trace of the picture they wanted. If they got a good trace, then all other children could use the trace pattern. They colored popcorn with cake coloring and put it on a string to decorate the tree. They used ribbons left over from someone's gift a year or two ago. All the children got a chance to do something when the tree was decorated. No one was left out.

We began practice on the school Christmas play several weeks before Christmas. We didn't take much time away from classes for this but everyone knew their lines and did well by the time for it to be presented. Christmas plays always had at least one that portrayed the Christmas story. Teachers were careful to include every child in some phase of the program.

The teacher picked some fat man from the community to

be Santa Claus. He came in at the very last of the program yelling Ho Ho Ho and carrying candy, oranges and apples in his bag. He was enjoyable to the little kids that thought there was a Santa Claus and also to those who knew there wasn't but wished there were. He handed out the treats to the kids, passed around a box of mixed candy for the parents and visitors, held and kissed all the little ones and kissed some of the mothers. They didn't seem to mind. In fact, they seemed to enjoy it. Everyone went away from the program full of candy and saying that this was the best program they had ever seen.

After all this Santa had another job he had to do. He went to the Christmas tree and took the gifts and read the name on it and the boy or girl would to come to him, hug his neck and get their gift. The gift was from a student that had drawn another student's name. The kids and teacher had written their names on a small piece of paper and put it in a box. Then the teacher passed the box around and everyone drew out a name. This had been done several weeks before. Some kids hated for some other kid to get their name because they knew they wouldn't get much. But they liked for some kid from a family that had a little more to get their name. This caused a sad situation at times but no one said much about it.

During the cold winter months around Christmas time, the teacher, who also acted as janitor, usually came to school a little early each morning and started a fire. Several of the students would already be there for their folks got up early and sent them on to school. To start a fire in a "pot-bellied"[9] stove or King Heater, the teacher put in an armload of kindling and then on top of that four or five sticks of dry firewood, usually oak or hickory and lit a paper and dropped it in the stove. If it didn't catch quickly, they threw in about a quart of coal oil and sometimes some daring crazy person threw in gasoline. This made the stove almost jump out of the room. It gave a big huff and roar and moved around some and the sides soon became red hot. Students would move close to it as soon as it got hot for they were cold and sometimes wet. They would stand and let one side get warm, then turn around and warm the other side. In real cold weather the teacher let the students sit in a circle around the stove so they could keep warm.

The one-room school had physical education the entire year. Students didn't need much exercise because they got plenty of that at home doing the chores and walking a long way to school. And many of their games during cold and hot weather were running games. But they didn't play alone. The teacher didn't just stand around and act as a guard or break up fights or do nothing. They played as hard as anyone. They played softball, rounder, cowboys and Indians and any running game that was played. It was not uncommon for a teacher, man or woman, to slide into second base, hit a home run, or peep out of a ditch with a wooden toy gun and say bang at someone they saw before being seen. They were just as active as the students and enjoyed being the pitcher, the catcher, the villain or doing anything the children wanted them to do. No parent questioned the supervision given students by the teacher because they knew that most of them would be out there on the playground doing just what the students were doing and dreading, just as much as the students were, for recess to be over.

Sometime during the third or fourth grade, young boys got a lesson outside the school building but they didn't know for awhile what it meant—the first time they saw the "four letter word," F--K. I remember seeing it on the back of an "outhouse" at a rural school. Some older students had carved it there. But whatever it was or whoever carved it or whoever saw it first, the word got around that it was there and most everyone went to look at it even if they did not know what it meant. At least a fourth grader didn't know. But it was strange and some way it was just bad and we didn't talk about it much. We just looked at it. The older kids said it had something to do with sex but that didn't mean anything to us except we knew it shouldn't be there and we shouldn't say it or talk about it. We didn't know why or how it was bad. We just knew. So we just continued to look at it.

Most of the older boys who were about eighteen or twenty knew much more about everything than a fourth grader. And sometimes they liked to tell the younger ones things they didn't need to know. But most of the little ones managed to survive and when they got to be eighteen they did the same thing to other little ones.

It was a happy time when the teacher told the students on Monday that on Friday they would have their pictures made in a group in front of the school house. A man who took pictures for a living would be there that day. So they told their parents what the teacher had said and if they had a new hat or ribbon for their hair, a new shirt or a new dress or anything new, they wore it on Friday. They wanted to look their best and their parents wanted them to look good.

In most rural schools the ages of the students ranged from six to above twenty. Sometimes the school board would allow a child four or five to go to school before the lawful age of six. And sometimes the board would allow students in their twenties to continue and take the eighth grade the second year.

The group picture above was made in 1907 at the Colvin School in Ozark County, Missouri. It was a one-room rural school, grades one to eight, with one teacher. The enrollment that year was small for some reason, about twenty. Often the number went to thirty-five or forty.

Several students went the second year because they hated the idea of quitting and they would not go on to high school. At that time there were no bus routes for many children who lived several miles from the high school and many parents did not have the money to pay "board and room" for an entire school year.

School was out about the middle of February. Sometimes it was out on Valentine's Day so students exchanged valentines that most of them had made and had written little verses on them. But whatever they did the last day was a big event because this was the day, the one day, that students didn't study much but played a lot and did some work for the teacher that needed to be done.

Usually the Mothers of the students would bring in food and treats for the children so the children didn't have to carry their little lard buckets of food to school that day. They sang songs and played games with the teacher and the parents.

About all the work they did was to place the books used during the year on shelves at the back of the room. They separated the books, dusted them good and placed one kind in one section. There were several books like spelling, arithmetic, geography, civics, English and health. They placed the few storybooks they had on different shelves. They were not catalogued because they didn't need to be. Students could find what book they wanted in a hurry and the teacher didn't know how to catalogue anyway.

Sometimes the teacher, with approval from the school board, would let students take books home to study and read during the summer. If someone was having a little trouble in arithmetic, they could take a book home and practice on whatever it was they needed to know. Some students liked to take a storybook home and read it over again because they had liked it so much. But sometimes the board would not allow this. If the books had not been treated well the summer before, they would often say no to taking books home.

During the school year the students took turns dusting the erasers. It seemed that a student had a good feeling and felt special if they were chosen to clean the erasers one day. But on this day, the last day, everyone had a chance. So they went to the well house, large trees and even on the back side of the schoolhouse and dusted away. There was something about this that made everyone want to do it. It may have been the smell of the chalk.

Another chore on this last day was putting all the pieces of chalk in a sack to be saved for the next year in case they didn't get to buy a new box. After the students picked out all the pieces, they took a rag and cleaned the chalk tray which had not been cleaned all year.

Taking the ashes out of the stove was a job that had to be done but not many students liked this. They shoveled the ashes out of the stove into a large bucket and took them outside to the ash pile, a place they had taken them all year. Or, they often took them to the our-door toilets and put them underneath. They thought this helped stop the smell.

Dusting all the student's desk was hard work because most teachers insisted that they would be free of any dust or crayon marks or dirt of any kind. In fact, students did more than just dust. They washed the desk with a damp cloth to remove any dirt. The teacher and the students took pride in leaving a schoolhouse as clean as they could.

Many students in rural schools went to school every day. As a reward for this the teacher would often give each one a silver dollar at the end of the year.

During the year if a student got all their spelling words correct for a month, the teacher gave them a reward, usually a yellow pencil which looked better than a "penny pencil" which had no color at all. They looked just like a small stick of pine wood.

On this day, the last day of the year, the students that had gotten all the spelling words correct for each month of school got two or three yellow pencils.

To make sure no one was left out, the teacher gave everyone some type of reward such as an eraser for their pencils.

All of this was a special event for the students and the parents. The students had to go to the front of the room and get their silver dollars or yellow pencils while their parents beamed with pride.

The last event was the drawing for the empty chalk box. It was a neat little box with a sliding lid. Everyone wanted it. So the teacher put numbers in the box on small pieces of paper and wrote a number on a piece of paper which she put in her desk. The student that drew the number from the box that was the same as the number on the paper in the teacher's desk got the box.

So, now, the school year was over. Some were glad but many were sad. They would miss their friends during the time from February to July.

Chapter XV

Folk History

<u>Murders</u>

When a murder was committed or someone died in a mysterious way, people talked about it for years. Some tried to solve it. Many pointed a finger at an innocent person but it was an excitement, a mystery which never left the community.

During the many years of Ozark Mountain history, men have been thrown in ponds, burned in haystacks, beaten with clubs, cut to death with a knife, shot point blank, shot from ambush, and beaten to death with brass knucks and killed in various other ways.

The murder rate in the Ozarks has been low compared to other sections of the country. I asked a resident one time if it was safe during the first part of the century for a stranger to move into the community. He said it was no problem most of the time since hill people do not often murder strangers; they murder their own people.

Reasons for murders were many. Disagreements over a fence line, dispute over who owned a cow or horse, jealously over a woman, the shooting of a man's dog, differences of opinion at a school election and too much corn whisky among other things have been considered causes.

Courts of law that try people for murder give strange decisions at times. In some counties a man will get a longer term in the "pen" for stealing a pig or shooting a dog than for killing a man. It all depends on the people who make up the jury. Some things are just more important than others to some people.

The following account of a murder and the reaction of the people was told to me by my father who was about fifteen years old when it happened. This would have been about 1910. He heard his father and brothers and other members of the community talk about it in the country store and any other place where they got a chance to talk.

Early in the 20th century the murder mystery of the old Sycamore Pond swept through the community of Dora, Missouri, in Ozark County and the surrounding area in Douglas County.

In Sycamore Pond near Richville, Missouri, a small community about eight miles north of Dora, two small boys were fishing one day. After they had fished for awhile, one of the boys pulled on his line and the leg of a man came out of the water.

A few weeks before this, a boy was staying with a family and hunting and trapping during the fur season, stole all the furs from a man with whom he was staying and left the county. The man who lost the furs was furious and went about the community saying that he would kill the boy if he ever saw him again.

Well, when a boy was found in the pond, the man who had made the statements about killing a boy was arrested and was about to be hanged by the angry people of the community. They even took the man to the pond one evening late where the boy had been found and asked him to identify the boy. The people were determined to see justice for the killing of a young boy was something they would not stand for. Immediately, the man knew he was in trouble.

He said that the boy who stole his furs had on a pair of blue overalls and a pair of "don't kick" shoes. They raised a leg from the pond water and there were the shoes and the blue overalls. The crowd had become a mob by now and became more angry at this and threatened to swing the man over a limb.

However, at that moment an old man in the crowd said that he had seen the boy who was accused of stealing the furs the night before. He said that he had stayed at his house. So this evidence freed the man who had made the threats.

While this was going on and they were pulling the body from the pond, one man got sick and went home. Some said that it was possible that he had killed the boy in the pond. However, the murder was never solved. No one knows today who killed the poor boy in the pond, but everybody likes to talk about it.

My grandmother, Tennessee Martin James, told me that after the Civil War bushwhackers came through the country near Dawt, Missouri, and caused a lot of trouble. She said her father was working around the house one day when several men came by and forced her father at gunpoint to ride off with them. His wife and several little children were afraid. They dreaded to see their father leave with these strange men. They waited for months, years for him to return but they heard nothing from or about him except someone found his large black hat not far from his home. There is no doubt that he was murdered by the men.

Tall Tales

The tall tale was a means by which people in this Ozark

Mountain country were able to boast, to exaggerate, and to get such pleasure for themselves and others. The country store, the flour mill or the courthouse were suitable locations for such exciting lore. Old men liked to tell tales of getting whippings at school, or extreme weather conditions and of great hunting adventures.

At the country store they sat around the "pot-bellied" stoves on nail kegs and "thrashed" their yarns and tales. While they talked, they played checkers and chewed their twist or asked someone for a few crumbs. They looked around at the "patent" medicine on the shelves, at the jar of ball gum of many colors, or watched the owner of the store fill the order of Sister Jones. They told their stories, they laughed, they spat, they relaxed and sometimes they yawned if a story didn't move along well. They were happy contented storytellers.

One of the group might have said that there was only two things that kept him from killing two big fat hogs that day for his meat. If someone asked him what the two things were, his answer would have been, just not having the hogs. Then they would all laugh.

To listen to these tales and stories was a pleasure. To have been a part of the storyteller's group was a greater pleasure.

A Tale of the Buck on Bald Knob Mountain

My grandfather told me this tale and insinuated that he was the brave hunter in the woods.

About 1900 a man went deer hunting one day. He decided that if he could climb a tree, he could see every deer within several hundred yards. Well, he climbed him a tree and stayed there for quite a spell, but saw no dear. But at about the time he was getting ready to get down and go home, he looked down to the ground and right there under him, under that very tree, was a big buck. He was the biggest buck he had ever laid eyes on.

He looked around, cocked his gun and aimed it right at the top of that buck's head. But the darned thing jammed. What on earth would he do? If he tried to unjam the gun, that big feller would knock the holler dry a'gettin' out of there.

Well, there wasn't but one thing to do. He'd have to jump down on that big feller and wear him down. So he eased down and around easy like, and jumped on that buck. Now that deer was scared. He ran and ran and bucked and snorted with that old boy hanging on for dear life. They wallered around there for several minutes and finally the old boy sorta "wared" him down a little and got a better grip on his horns. But that didn't help much. Finally, the old boy saw that he wasn't getting' no where so he grabbed a handful of red clay and stuffed it in that buck's nose and by Ned smothered that big feller to death. And he didn't have a scratch on him from workin' on that deer. He's got the head and the horns over his fireplace jest to show he dun it.

A Tale of the Three Who Went West

My father and uncles told this tale to me and anyone else that would listen.

Alva Harrison, Ben Hargin and Ely Croan were hard working Ozark hill farmers. They were respected by their neighbors and thought to be honest men. They were, as some say in the Ozarks, "Hard workin', poor folks."

When the three were seen with plenty of silver money, people began to wonder how on earth they got so much. The talk of their sudden fortune soon spread throughout the neighborhood and everyone became curious and began to "eye" every move they made.

Finally, it was reported by Beth Simpson, wife of Harley Simpson, who was a distant cousin of Ben Hargin, an honest church attender, that she had seen the three making trips West, often. All the neighbors began to take notice and talk about her statements.

These trips went on for several years. Finally, when the government agents came in to investigate a report of counterfeiters in the area, the three were arrested.

They were tried in court and the government proved that they had silver dollars that were not United States currency. But the men kept quiet and nothing else was proved. The jury set them free.

One by one the men finally died and the mystery was never solved. But it is said that the community knows the sly way that Alva, Ben and Ely took the good country for several thousand dollars.

Horns and a Dilemma

This story was told to me by Donald Clem of Fairfield Bay, Arkansas as a true story that happened on his boyhood farm. I am including it in this section of tall tales because one can imagine the delight that people could enjoy as they retold this story time after time.

The horns mentioned in the title belonged to a calf named Princess. Her mother had died not long after she was born. It seems that Princess and her owners had trouble from then on.

"Since Princess was born in November, she was kept in the kitchen beside the coal fired stove. To add to the difficulties she was bottle fed until strong enough to be placed in the pen with other calves. Princess apparently began to look at herself as part of the family if her actions were any indication. She wanted food from the table, especially apples, oranges and sugar. Of course, the youngest of the family obliged and fed her. It was better than listening to her moo if she wasn't given food."

After being relegated to the calf pen she continued to want human companionship. When her humans were outside, she would follow them around when the opportunity was present. One activity that she liked was to watch the farmer's kids pump water for her four footed friends. The pump, an old fashioned type which had a long handle, was on a platform which was about four feet on a side. The platform had a railing which encompassed the four sides. When the calf's humans pumped water, the calf would place her hooves on the platform, extended her head and neck over the railing to get her face scratched and receive any offerings of apples, sugar or other goodies. When the calf heard the pump rattle, she would come running. The farmer's kids enjoyed the calf as much as the calf enjoyed the kids, or so it seemed."

"One late spring day the farmer's wife told one of the kids to pump water for the other beasts. The child came back and told his mother that the trough was full. His mother allowed as how one of the other children must have pumped the water before they left with their father. No more thought was given to the event."

"Some time later when the farmer went to pump water he found a full trough. He assumed that one of the children had pumped the water but the kids usually had to be instructed to fill the trough, so he was somewhat puzzled. Over the days the trough would mysteriously be filled but the family members insisted that it had not been any of them who pumped the water."

"The mystery was solved when the farmer's wife caught the culprit. Everyone but the farmer's wife was gone that afternoon. She heard the pump rattling and looked out the kitchen window. There was that eight-month-old calf with her front hooves on the platform. Her head and neck were extended over the railing. She placed the horn on the right side (her horns were now about twelve inches long) under the handle and pushed it up. Then she placed her chin on top of the handle and pushed it down. After several strokes she would go down and look at the trough. If there wasn't enough water to suit her, she would go back to pumping. Of course, she ran the trough over but that didn't seem to be of any concern to her. During the remaining four months the farmer owned her the trough was seldom empty."

"The old pump would lose its prime from time to time. Princess would run the handle up and down with no results but when the family heard the pump one of them would check to make sure there was water coming out. If not, the pump would be primed so that Princess would not labor in vain."

"One time the farmer took a delivery of concrete blocks which were to be used to make a foundation for the barn. The blocks were stacked in the barnyard where the animals roamed since animals don't know anything about concrete blocks. The block stacks were about four feet high and some of the block holes were turned out instead of up. That is where the trouble started. In fact, the farmer's two boys came close to getting strapped over these blocks."

"The farmer came home one afternoon and found concrete blocks scattered all over the barn yard. He accused his sons of the deed but they insisted they had not done so. The farmer's wife said the boys didn't do it, so the mystery remained. The farmer placed the blocks back on the stacks but the next morning more blocks were scattered about."

"Now that was a sure enough mystery but the solution was soon forthcoming. The family heard a noise one evening that sounded like the blocks being moved against each other. They went to look. Do you need three guesses as to what they found? If you said Princess, you are correct. Princess would walk up to a stack and stick a horn into a block hole. She would lift the block and let it swing on the horn. She would then turn around and repeat the procedure with the empty horn. After loading both horns, she would walk off and drop the blocks several feet from the stack. She continued until she could find no more blocks with accessible holes. The farmer returned the blocks to the stacks but turned the hole up so they were horn proof. As smart as Princess seemed to be she just refused to put the blocks back on the stacks."

"The last straw with this intelligent animal came when she autographed the fresh concrete in the milking parlor. She left her hoof prints for all to see which did not please the farmer in the least. Princess had learned to unlatch gate hooks but no thought was given to her being able to unlatch the slatted door to the milking area. Since the hook was on the inside, the only way to unlock the door was to reach between the last two slats nearest the opening edge. Princess had watched the farm family do that many times as she watched everything else they did."

"When the farmer found that she had been in the concrete he assumed that the gate had been left unlocked. He fixed the concrete and locked the gate. A few minutes later after leaving the barn, Princess was seen standing at the slatted door. She stuck her horn between those slats, twisted her head counter clockwise, and unlatched that hook as smartly as you please. By the time she started to set hooves into the fresh concrete again the farmer was there to chase her away. He latched the gate and watched. She came back and repeated her act. After chasing her away, the farmer used some bailing wire to secure the door. Princess worked for several minutes on the hook but when she was not successful she went out to the pasture."

"The farmer found a buyer for Princess. It was just as well as I look back on these events. The well went dry; the blocks were used for the foundation; and the concrete became hard. There was no longer anything for Princess to do so she had to go to greener pastures. Perhaps another farmer could use her skills. But if you were to look in the milking parlor of that barn, you would see a hoof print of the smartest calf I have ever known. When my dad fixed the floor, he left one of her prints. If you look real close, you will see the date etched faintly in the concrete. I am sure the people who now own that farm do not know the origin and history of that hoof print. They probably wouldn't believe the story if they were told."

Chapter 16

The Supernatural

There are some things people just do not do in the Ozarks. There are "hainted" places that people do not enjoy being near. Some people consider it taboo to walk under a ladder or cross the path of a black cat at any time. Many people will drive their car into the ditch to avoid a black cat.

Again, as is the case in other types of lore, the supernatural beliefs are community and family ideas. Some are thought to be silly in one community or family and respected seriously in another.

Many of the beliefs are about the subject of death. Yet good luck and bad luck are close seconds. The strangest beliefs are those concerning the marking of babies before birth and blood stoppers.

The ghost story, like a superstition, is restricted to certain communities. An old house may be "hainted" or a graveyard may have many ghosts around it. A dark valley may be a place where ghosts and strange figures are seen every night. Some people in some areas seem to enjoy the ghost in their midst. Some laugh at the idea.

It must be understood that stories of the supernatural are not found just in the Ozarks. Similar stories may be told in different regions of a state or even in a different state.

Beliefs

My grandmother knew all the old beliefs, it seemed. She often told me not to do this or that or do this or that or I would have bad luck. I often listened to her conversations with other women concerning blood stopping, marked babies, water witching and signs of good or evil. I liked to listen to them talk for they had their own opinions and didn't care to voice them. When a certain lady in our community came to visit her, I knew that they would talk a lot about beliefs and how they had harmed or helped someone so I got me a comfortable place to lie down and listen. It was enjoyable and I never forgot what I heard.

One of the beliefs in the Ozarks which is related to the supernatural is water witching. It is an art that only a few people have the ability to do but many would like to know how.

The water witcher has only one piece of equipment. This is a forked stick out from an elm or peach tree. It is held by grasping the two pointed ends in an "over-handed" way. After grasping the stick the witcher is ready to find water.

When the stick is over water, it begins to "bobble" or pull down. If there is a strong stream of water the stick almost jumps or twists out of the witcher's hands. The manner in which a stick moves up and down indicates within a few feet the distance it is to the underground stream of water.

People in other parts of the United States have heir own ideas of how the stick will react to water.

Many people never drill a well without doing some work and investigation with a well-known "witcher." If the "witcher" says the driller should drill in the front yard or under the house, that is the place he must drill. Some drillers hate the sound of a man's name who says he can find water. They have had the experience of drilling many dry holes because of some "quack witcher" who didn't know his way around. The man who says he can find water is known by many unusual names in the drilling business.

But if you want an argument, just tell a "witcher" that he is just trying to do something that can not be done. He will inform you that he has been one hundred percent correct in all his attempts to find water. And in addition to that, he got the power from his father who got it from his grandfather. If you continue to dispute his ability, you will be hurting his family pride. The only thing to do is to agree with him and try to find your water with an elm or peach tree stick.

The following is a list of superstitions that my grandmother and other people in the Ozarks have told me:
- If you eat black-eyed peas on New Years, you will have good luck all year.
- It is bad luck to sweep under a sick bed.
- If you throw one big apple peeling over your shoulder, it will form the initial of your future mate.
- If you drop a fork while doing dishes, it means a man is coming.
- It is bad luck to put a hat on while you are in bed.
- If someone sends you a Christmas card before you send them one, you may have bad luck.
- When you start somewhere, don't turn back. It is bad luck.
- Don't tell your dream before breakfast or it will not come true.
- Do not open an umbrella in the house. It is bad luck.
- If you break a mirror, you will have seven years of bad luck.

- If a coal oil lamp runs out of oil, there will be a death in the family.
- If your dog whines at night, it means a death will happen in the family.
- Never bring an ax in the house. It is bad luck.
- Don't ever give away anything sharp. It will cut your friendship.
- Two people should never go around a post, one on each side. This will cause very bad luck. They should go around on the same side.
- Never let a cat into a baby's room. Sometimes it will take the baby's breath.
- If you find an old horseshoe, hang it on a limb for good luck.
- If a bird flies into the house, there will be bad luck for someone.
- Never rock an empty cradle. It is a sign of death.
- Never tickle a baby under the chin. If you do, it will stutter.
- Wash a baby's head in stump water and it will never be bald.
- If you carry out ashes on New Years, you will carry out a member of your family before the year is over.
- Never sing before breakfast or you will cry before bed time.
- Never sweep under anyone's feet.
- Never step over anyone lying on the floor.
- If you set out a cedar tree before it gets big enough to shade you, it will die before it makes a shade.
- When a chicken flies to roost and crows, there will be trouble in the family.
- If your rooster crows on the doorstep, you will have company soon.
- The number of times you can skip a rock across water will be the number of children you will have.
- If you eat cherry pie and drink milk at the same time, you will become very sick and may die.

- If a dog rolls in front of you three times, you will hear of a death in three days.
- Never point your finger at lightning. If you do, it may strike you.
- Don't eat fish and drink milk together. It will make you sick and you may die.
- If a hen crows, it is a sign of bad luck.
- If you spin a chair around on its leg, there will be a death in the family.
- If you do not put your tongue in the hole where you have pulled a tooth, a gold tooth will grow there.
- Throw salt over your left shoulder for good luck.
- If you sleep on your stomach, you will dream of food.
- If a black cat comes to your house, don't get rid of it yourself or you will have bad luck.
- When a star falls, someone dies.
- When it rains during a funeral, the Angels in Heaven are weeping.
- Don't leave a diaper in someone's house. It will bring a baby there.
- Don't kill a snake on Sunday or you will see one every day that week.

Ghost Stories

If you have visited a haunted house, you have heard the roar and rumble upstairs. You have heard the squeak, the scrape, the scratch and the almost silent walk of the mysterious stranger in the white gown.

If you have ever sat down with a teller of ghost stories in a dark room, you have experienced the haunting feeling of being slipped up on from behind. You have listened to them tell of those who came back from the grave, or those who travel around in sleepy hollows on white horses, and of those who will disappear into the dark woods on a rainy night.

If you have known a person who really believed in ghosts, you know that no amount of argument can make them admit that they have never seen a ghost.

Ghosts are seen everywhere in the Ozarks but they seem to prefer graveyards, old abandoned houses, lonely wooded areas and deserted roadways. No doubt their favorite of all places is in or near a graveyard. There they rise up from the grave at the hour of midnight and make their rounds over the country. They seem to delight in frightening young lovers who walk home from a party or an old man who can not run very fast.

I have heard my father and other men tell a story about a man who was chased by a ghost for several miles. Finally the poor man became tired and could run no longer.

When he stopped, the ghost placed his hand on the man's shoulder and said, "That was some going, old boy."

The scared man looked around into the face of the ghost and replied, "Yes sir, and we's goin' to go some more."

The following accounts of ghosts have been told and retold throughout the Ozarks for many years. They have been enjoyed by some but they have scared the "daylights" out of others.

My father told me the following story, "The Ghost at Rocky Crossin'." He had been raised around Dora, Missouri where there are several graveyards and small streams and branches. This environment may have given him a greater interest in the story.

<u>The Ghost at Rocky Crossin'</u> It had been raining for seven long days and nights. The days and nights were unusually dark. The sun had not been seen during the long gloomy week. The streams and branches were out of their banks

and tree frogs croaked for more of the same. The neighbors made comments about the unusual weather in July. "More rain, more rest, more workers in the west," they said, and in spite of the weather, a revival meeting at a rural church in the Dawt, Missouri community went on as planned.

Now one of the young men of this community, Jim Ross, who was seeking romantic ties, was attending church every night. About halfway between his home and the church was a graveyard. Every time he passed the graveyard he had an urge to spur his horse. He even looked back over his shoulder to see if anything was there behind.

This night seemed to be no darker than any before, yet the rain had formed into a fine mist. It was difficult to see five feet in front of the horse. But there was something strange about everything as Jim approached the graveyard that night. He seemed to be expecting something. Just before he reached the road which led to the graveyard gate, he saw a glare of light ahead of him. The object seemed to be going up and down, up and down. It came nearer, then vanished, then appeared again, even closer. Scared as stiff as a dead rabbit, Ross just stood his horse there and nothing happened for several minutes. He decided that he had been seeing things and started to go on by. Suddenly the white figure rose eight or ten feet in the air and slowly moved to the northeastern corner of the graveyard and seemed to go down into a grave.

By this time, Ross was scared out of his wits. He ran his horse with all his might the rest of the way home. He didn't even take time to remove the saddle, just left the horse standing at the gate. He said that he didn't get comfortable until daylight the next morning. He didn't tell his girl friend about this for years after they were married. He was afraid that she would think he was sorta silly and not believe him but even today he thinks of that dark night and what he saw and how scared he was.

<u>The Old Haint</u> Near the community of Caulfield, Missouri, sometime during the 1930s people believed they had a witch or ghost of some type at work. I heard this story in the 1940s when I was going to school at nearby Bakersfield, Missouri.

It seems that every morning when one family's cow came to the barn to be milked, there would be a spotted deer with it. The deer would stay with the cow and would not let her go into the barn. Despite all the farmer could do the deer was always there to bother the poor cow.

Some of the people finally told the man to shoot the deer with a silver bullet and the deer would turn into what it was supposed to be. So the farmer thought it over and decided that was what he should do.

So he made a bullet from a silver dollar and the next evening shot the deer in the leg. The neighbors followed the bloodstains through the woods. They led to an old woman's house who had been unfriendly with everyone for several years. In fact, she would not let anyone in her house. She was a witch to many people. Some said that she turned into a ghost at night. But this time the neighbors were determined to go into her house since the blood of the deer led there. And there was the old woman bleeding from a bullet hole in her leg. The people left as soon as they could for they knew they had found out what she was. They had been right all the time. Witches and ghosts did come in the form of animals and harm people and their property. Now they would be careful what they said to certain people they suspected.

No one in the community had any more trouble with the spotted deer.

Max Decker, Ed. D.

<u>Ghost or no Ghost</u> My mother, Gladys Martin Decker, told me this story when I was a small child and I never forgot it.

Many people have heard strange noises and seen strange sights which proved to be something other than ghosts.

One time, two men were coming home from church. As they passed an old house near a dark hollow, they heard a strange noise inside. They rode as fast as they could. They went home and got their guns and returned to the house. They crept up as quietly as possible and knocked down the door. They were ready to catch the old ghost. After they got into the old house, they found an old sow and her pigs cracking hickory nuts. They were, indeed, strange looking ghosts.

Mother also told me that one time there were three men who went fox hunting one night. As they passed an old house, they heard a terrible noise that scared them almost "to death." No one lived in the house which caused them to be scared even more. Finally, they got enough nerve to go in and investigate. They found that the noise had been the work of several pack rats in the attic.

But even if other things sound like ghosts might, it is impossible to make a man of the hills comfortable near a graveyard at night or in a house that people have said was haunted.

<u>The Haunted House</u> Alice Lirley who lives in the Red Bank community of Douglas County, Missouri told me several ghost stories that people around Red Bank and Goodhope in Douglas County had told over and over for years. She also told some interesting stories from the Bradleyville area in Taney County, Missouri.

Once there was a man who offered fifty dollars to anyone who would stay all night in a house that everyone thought was inhabited by ghosts. Now there was a preacher in the community that hadn't been paid very well by the members of his church and he needed money. So he decided to stay. He went into the old house and shut the door.

He said, "No ghost will get me, no not one." But as he said these words a ghost stepped out.

He went to the fireplace and placed a board over it and said, "No ghost will get me now." But out of the chimney came a ghost.

He raised the window and slammed it shut and said, "No ghost will get me now." But out stepped a ghost.

He saw that these things were doing no good so he started praying. But several ghost came after him. He started singing but the ghost came on. He started shouting but the ghost was still there.

Finally, he started passing his hat for a collection and the ghost all left.

<u>The Singing Kettle</u> An old farm lady had a large black kettle in her back yard in which she made hominy and soap. At times she said she thought it was a ghost because she could hear it singing. When this happened, she said someone died.

<u>Rappins</u> Mrs. Lirley said that her stepfather, Lorie Maggard, told a story about the experiences of a man after his wife died. The man had gone to bed when suddenly he woke up and thought he heard something. It sounded like a knock at his door. He sat up in bed and listened carefully. The knock went rap, rap, rap. He asked in a scared voice, "Who is knocking at my door?" But there was still no reply.

With fear and trembling in his voice he got enough courage to call out the name of his deceased wife.

"Roda," he called. "If that is you knocking at the door, let me know by knocking four times instead of three." After what seemed like a long time to him, there came a loud rap, rap, rap, rap.

That answer seemed to shake the old boy up pretty bad. He was ready to move out of the house. He didn't seem to be ready for a visit from the ghost of his deceased wife now or anytime in the future. He told many people about his experience that night and convinced many that his deceased wife had returned.

The House Haunted by a Headless Ghost Mrs. Lirley's mother, Rocca Maggard, was born in 1911 on a farm about three miles from Brown Branch, Missouri. She was married at the age of sixteen and she and her husband moved into a little one-room log house about three and one-half miles below Brandeyville, Missouri on Brushy Creek.

According to Mrs. Maggard one could go about a mile and one-half from where they lived up an old canyon road to an old house that many people thought was haunted. It is said that there was a big dance party at the house many years before and that the owner of the house was murdered. It seemed that the man's head was severed when a big fight broke out during the party.

Mrs. Maggard said that since then no one would go near the house. Several people who went by the house after the terrible murder reported that they had seen a headless man standing in the doorway draped in white.

But as a young lady Mrs. Maggard had got close enough to the old house one time to spy an apple tree in the back yard just full of beautiful red apples. Her mouth watered for those red apples. She knew that she could also can a few quarts of them.

She told her good husband about the apples and he warned her to stay away from that haunted house. It seemed that everyone in the community knew about the apples but no one would pick them for fear of the headless ghost.

She was of a strong headed nature and wanted those apples so she decided to check out the story that she had always heard about the ghost. She remembered her mother telling her one time that if she was ever confronted by a ghost to just talk to it and ask it what it wanted and why it was there and it would probably leave her alone.

So one afternoon she saddled her horse, found a couple of "toesacks," and began to ride down the canyon trail toward the old haunted house.

As she got nearer the house, she saw nothing standing in the doorway. She slowly rode closer and closer expecting to see the ghost at any time. She was scared. She gripped the reins tighter for fear the ghost might spook the horse. She rode closer and soon was directly in front of the porch and doorway. There was no ghost yet but her heart began to pump harder as she got out of the saddle. She carefully stepped on the old porch. She noticed that there was no door. It had probably been torn down the time of the fight that caused the terrible murder.

As she stepped inside the doorway, all she could see was the big bloodstains on the floor which were probably left by the murdered man. She walked slowly, and listened carefully for any noise. Her body was ready to react to the slightest movement. But there was no noise.

So she decided to try her luck for some of those apples she had seen in the backyard. She led her horse carefully around to the back of the house. She filled both of the "toesacks" with apples, slung one behind her and the saddle seat and one between her and the old saddle horn and rode toward home. She said that she did not find one worm in those apples as she cut them up and canned them for the winter's use.

<u>Rail Fence Ghost</u> Not far from Mrs. Lirley's mother's house was another place that people from miles around said was haunted. Every moonlit night around midnight people could see a man dressed in white sitting on a fence in the backyard.

Her mother's young husband said he had witnessed this very sight and told her to stay away from there.

But curiosity got the best of her mother and she asked her husband to go with her to see the ghost. So on the first moonlit night they saddled their horses and rode toward the old house place that was on the top of a long hill.

When they got within about two hundred feet of the house, her husband announced that that was as far as he was going. But she said, "Suit yourself but I am going to talk to that old ghost and ask it why it was sitting on the fence like that."

She carefully inched her way around the back of the house and there it was, the ghost of a man dressed in white sitting on the fence. She was startled to say the least. Should she approach the ghost or go back to her husband and take off for home?

She knew she could never stand the teasing she would have to take so she had to keep on going. She inched her way on until she was almost directly in front of the ghost on the fence. As she got closer, she noticed she could see only a part of man. She went closer and the ghost almost disappeared. She looked all around. As she looked behind her, she could see the moon shining through the limbs of the poplar trees. When she stepped back from the beams of light, she again saw the man sitting on the fence, dressed in white.

Immediately she rejoined her husband and told him what she had found but she never did convince him to look for himself. He still believed the old house place was haunted by a man dressed in white sitting on the backyard fence.

<u>The Church Place Ghost</u> Mrs. Lirley's stepfather, Lorie Maggard, told a story about a ghost light that he and another person observed in about 1935.

He said he and another man were on their way home from church services at the Mt. Olive Church one evening. This is in the western part of Douglas County, Missouri. It is called the Highlonesome area.

They were riding their horses side by side down the middle of the road. As they came to the top of the long hill where the Eastern Gate Church sets today, but which was not built at that time, the horses stopped still at the sight of what looked like a young boy with very large hands. The boy seemed to be surrounded by a bright light and he walked out and stood in front of them.

Mr. Maggard's horse raised his front right leg to paw at the image. But there was no solid mass touched by the horse's foot. It was pawing at the thin air and bright light.

He said he slipped off his horse to try to catch what he thought was a boy, but the image moved around the horse and seemed to enter the horse's body. Soon the light disappeared.

Bewildered by the strange events the young men continued on their way home.

As they traveled by another area that is now the building site of the Breedon Church, the light appeared again but disappeared as fast as it came.

They did not realize that this was not the last time that the bright light would appear to them so they followed the old country road that led to the Red Bank Store that was in the exact spot where the Red Bank Church is now. Again the light appeared but it vanished again.

The men told their story to their neighbors and their parents and anyone who would listen. They told several fox hunters who became interested in the bright light and went into the woods with their fox hounds to try to find some evidence of the glowing ghost, but they found nothing.

It seemed strange to the young men that everywhere the ghost light appeared, a church was built not long after the sighting.

Several people including the men said they believed the light was really the ghost of someone murdered in that area. Mr. Maggard said his father told him that it might have been the ghost of a man who had been murdered by another man who had just been released from prison. For some reason he was jealous of an old man he had employed to help with chores while he was in prison. The ex-convict hit the old man right between the eyes with his fist and he fell dead. This was about the same place that they saw the bright light.

The Man-Eating Booger of Booger County   Mrs. Alice Lirley told me that her aunt told her about an incident that she could never forget. It seems that many people including her aunt's father was fond of telling chilling stories of being chased by a big hungry animal or some type of "booger" as they called them.

One time her aunt and some other people were chased by a large man-eating animal or booger. They ran for safety inside their house. They barely got the door shut when they heard the thud of the animal's head hitting the door. It was snarling, scratching and pawing. They believed it was ready to make a tasty meal out of them.

Another time some members of the same family decided to go possum hunting with their grandpa's old dog by their side. They didn't take a gun but they did take a big club. All they needed was the club to hit the possum over the head when they found it. They knew that possums would be still and appear to be dead. When they do this, the hunters can hit them over the head with the club. This action of the possum is where the term "playing possum" comes from.

They walked quietly down the holler looking for the possum. It was dark but they had gone quite a way when all of a sudden they heard a strange sound in the distance. Whosha, whosha, whosha it sounded.

Immediately they began to think of the stories they had been told about the "booger" so they decided to go back to the house.

Suddenly they heard the sound again. Whosha, whosha, whosha it went. Their hearts began to beat faster and louder. Their footsteps got quicker. The further they went, the louder and closer the sound became. The closer they got to the house, the louder the sound became. They couldn't understand that.

Their eyes got as big as saucers and cold chills ran up their backs as they broke into a full run. The sound became so loud to them that they could almost feel the hot breath of the fierce animal against their backs.

As they broke through the timber into the clearing where the log house stood, they looked for the door that meant possible escape from the "booger" or terrible animal. But all they could see was the outline of someone in front of the house. But they did not know who it could be.

A few feet more and they could finally make it to the dark image that stood between them and the door to safety.

Soon they found that that dreadful sound that had been nipping at their heels was Grandpa standing outside shaking a big dishpan full of hot peanuts he had just roasted. He was cooling them off in the cool night air-- Whosha, whosha, whosha!

Telling Your Fortune

The following ways to tell your fortune was exciting to rural school children and to some adults.

When people made coffee in a can and some of the coffee grounds were left, they used this as a way to tell their fortune. After someone drank their coffee, they shook and twisted their cup to make a design in the bottom of the cup. They thought that the design that was left told them something about their future. Yet, whatever they saw in the cup was their own imagination. They made their fortune whatever they wanted.

Dragonflies were used to tell fortunes. They were found over still water like ponds. Parents told their children to be careful when they saw them because snakes would be nearby. So the children were afraid and called them Snakefeeders. They were also told that if they saw many in a small area, they would have bad luck for a year.

Water Striders and Whirligig Beetles moved in fast motion on top of the water. But they moved in no certain pattern. Children were told that if they watched these insects long enough, they would write their name, and maybe, if you were lucky, tell your future. Some children, including my daughter, Becky, would watch for hours trying to see their names in the patterns. They were a mystery to children and some adults. If they wrote your name, you would have good luck for at least a year.

Marked Babies

Although people enjoyed these and other ghost stories, some took them with "a grain of salt." But the problems of pregnant women were different.

Many people in the Ozarks believed that babies could be marked before they were born. If something unusual happened to the mother, especially during the first three months of pregnancy, just about anything could happen to the baby.

It is said that one time in the Ozarks a woman was hit by a ripe peach as she walked under the tree. When the baby was born, it had a spot on its arm the size and color of a peach. The spot became the color of a ripe peach during the time of year when peaches get ripe.

One woman who was two months pregnant suddenly stepped on a goat hide at a neighbor's house. She was frightened. When the baby was born, it had the form of a goat hide on its chest. The hair which grew on this place on the child's chest was like the hair on a goat.

One time a woman fell over a black calf before her baby was born. The baby had a black spot of hair on the top of its head.

Once, a cat bit a pregnant woman on the hand. When her baby was born, it had two red dots which looked like a cat bite on its hand.

Max Decker, Ed. D.

It was a belief in the Ozarks that pregnant women crave pickles. However, when a man whose wife was pregnant began to eat all the pickles he could find, no one knew what to believe.

Endnotes

[1] Apocryphal anecdote

[2] Apocryphal anecdote

[3] A by-product of ground wheat

[4] Civilian Conservation Corps

[5] This happened in a rural farmhouse near Tecumseh, Missouri about 1941.

[6] This bird is about the size and color as a Chickadee. People in the Ozarks often called them Pee Wee.

[7] Hill people referred to the signs of the Zodiac when they planted. For example, potatoes planted in a certain sign caused them to be all vine and few potatoes.

[8] Mashed potatoes pressed into a flat shape and fried. Most people made them about the size of their hand.

[9] A bag made of coarse jute sometimes called a gunny sack.

[10] A stove that was much larger at the bottom so it would hold more wood.

Sources, Notes and Information

Two of the major sources of the material found in this collection have come from my grandmother Tennessee James Martin (1860-1940) and from my life that I have lived in the Ozarks (1929-present)

She lived in a time when such things as remedies, times for planting and signs of the weather were necessary to know if people survived. Also she lived in a time when mysterious places and events were welcomed if they didn't hurt anyone, when church activities were an important part of many people's lives and when folk history, the supernatural and entertainment were important to her and many of her neighbors.

I lived in a time that was influenced by the Great Depression. Many of us were poor but we didn't know it. We wore what we had. We ate what we grew. The Depression didn't bother us too much. It just forced the rest of the country to live like most of us had always lived.

Introduction 1

Chapter 1--The Setting, The Country, The People 9
    Personal conversations and experiences of this writer

Chapter 2--Mysterious Places and Events 13

Sweetin Pond 14

    Decker, Jonathan, (1855-1946)
    Birdtown, Missouri

    Decker, E.C. (1895-1990)
    Tecumseh, Missouri

    Personal conversations by this writer

Taylor's Cave 15

    Martin, Tennessee James (1860-1941)
    Dawt, Missouri

    Personal conversations by this writer

The Horse Thief 17

    Decker, E.C. (1895-1990)
    Tecumseh, Missouri

    Owens, Charlie (1887-1984)
    Gainesville and Ava, Missouri

The Blue Man or Wild Man of the Ozarks 20

    Decker, E.C. (1895-1990)
    Tecumseh, Missouri

Chapter 3--Ozark Individuals 25

Depression time in the Ozarks 26

    Field, Maxine
    Mtn. View, Arkansas

    Personal conversations and experiences of this writer.

Peddlers 34

    Personal experiences of this writer

Drummers 36

Decker, Mona Gaulding
Nottinghill and Ava, Missouri

Personal experiences of this writer

Tramps 37

Personal experiences of this writer

Outlaws 37

Personal experiences of this writer

Preachers 38

Decker, Gladys Martin, (1899-1966)
Tecumseh, Missouri

Decker, Mona Gaulding
Nottinghill and Ava, Missouri

Martin, Tennessee James, (1860-1941)
Dawt, Missouri

Candidates for office 42

Decker, Jonathan, (1855-1946)
Birdtown, Missouri

Decker, E.C. (1895-1990)
Tecumseh, Missouri

Granny-Women 45

Personal experiences of this writer

Ozark Mountain Doctors and Dentists 45

Decker, E.C. (1895-1990)
Tecumseh, Missouri

Gaulding, Amy, ((1899-1980)
Nottinghill and Ava, Missouri

Personal experiences of this writer

Chapter 4--Childlore 55

Autograph verses..55
Collected from autograph books of students with whom I attended rural school at Colvin School in Ozark County, Missouri and from students that I taught at Dawt School in Ozark County, Missouri.

Most of these autograph verses came from many areas of the Ozarks because they traveled quickly by word-of-mouth

Games 66
These activity games and marble games were played by my students and me during the 30s and 40s. Some games such as "Bluejay" were played by adults. Teachers in rural schools played all the games with the children. Most of the games had different rules from one school to another and from one county to another. A major reason for this was that students made their own rules to suit themselves.

Marbles 82
As a rural school student and rural school teacher, I helped draw lines in the dirt so we could have a marble game. The games were interesting and the marbles had a beautiful color. Many students kept their marbles for years. In fact, I have several of the marbles I used almost sixty years ago.

Choosing Up 90
This was the way we had two sides. I learned much about choosing up since we did this every time we played a game that needed two sides.

Chapter 5--Folksay 91
Sayings 91

A saying is just words, phrases and statements that people in the Ozarks use to get their point across in conversation. No one knows for sure where they came from or when they came. They are just spoken when the speaker thinks they are right to use to make the person to whom they are speaking understand them better. It seems that people think they add a little color to their speech. Some may have originated in the Ozarks and some in other areas. The major source of these sayings is from personal conversations I have had over the years with people.

Bywords 97
Some bywords were used as fillers; some were used to show delight; some were said in disgust and some were just habit.

Mispronunciations 99
These words were heard by this writer over the years in conversations with people. Some people maybe didn't know any better but to most of them it was an easier way to say something and soon became a habit.

Comparisons 99
The source is personal conversations I have had as I talked to people in the Ozarks. Most people liked to exaggerate in their conversations. They could do that by making a comparison, usually in the form of a simile but it became a hyperbole as they finished it. These comparisons made it easier for people to communicate.

Conversations 102
Most people in the Ozarks liked to talk about almost anything. Their talk was filled with filler which the listener took as an encouragement for what they

were saying. A short one-word statement let the speaker know you were listening.

The source was my personal experience.

Place Names 104
The source for place names was Elmer Peterson of Norwood, Missouri who knew all the names of the school districts in Douglas County, Missouri and many in other parts of the Ozarks and my own information I got by traveling over the Ozarks all my life. Schools, towns, communities and post offices had names that were given them when they were established. Many names came from nature, such as Black Oak or Beaver.

Local Journalism 109
Local journalism contained some of the best creative writing in the Ozarks. The "items" let everyone know everybody's business and told of special events that might be of interest to someone.

The editor of the paper in which the "items" appeared did their best to correct mistakes and "cut out" unsuitable material but many times they did not do a very good job.

My major source for local journalism was my reading of what some people, mostly women, wrote about the rest of us.

Chapter 6--Epitaphs 113
Personal research by this writer

Chapter 7--Remedies 123
Martin, Tennessee James (1860-1941)
Dawt, Missouri

McClendon, Frank
Gainesville, Missouri

Personal experiences of this writer

Remedies were what saved lives in the Ozarks where there were few doctors and these few were miles away. I was told many of these remedies by my grandmother, Tennessee James Martin (1860-1941) of Dawt, Missouri. She told them to me from time to time until she died when I was eleven years old. I got a better understanding of them because when I got sick she made use of them on me. "Why are you feeding me that burned bread," I would ask her. "For your sick stomach," she would say. "It will be gone in a little while. But you may need a laxative. May give you some senna tea if it don't get better," she would say. She had been told many of the remedies by her parents and older brothers and sisters when they lived in Tennessee. So all the remedies were not peculiar to the Ozarks.

Chapter 8--Times for Planting.................................... 133

Decker, Gladys Martin, (1899-1966)
Tecumseh, Missouri

Martin, Tennessee James, (1860-1941)
Dawt, Missouri

They planted gardens and "truck patches" and maybe a separate area for potatoes. Many of the planting beliefs had been brought from Tennessee and Kentucky and other states when they came to the Ozarks. They watched the signs of the Zodiac and the moon. Their machinery was primitive compared to that of today. They made most of their tools in the blacksmith shop. They used their own horses and mules for power. But they raised enough to feed their families and they ate well. They bought only staples at the grocery store. They ate many things filled with grease but that didn't seem to bother them. No doubt they burned up the grease by getting up at 4:00 o'clock in the morning and working until the sun went down. They knew how to make a garden. They knew how to fight the bugs and keep the rabbits out. They grew enough to give to their neighbors who didn't have something and the neighbors did the same.

Chapter 9--Signs of the Weather 143

Decker, Gladys Martin, (1899-1996)
Tecumseh, Missouri

Martin, Tennessee James (1860-1941)
Dawt, Missouri

Personal conversations of this writer

Before the time of the radio in the Ozarks, people did not have much information about the weather. The U.S. Weather Bureau brought the "weatherman" when we finally got radios. This helped people with their forecast. But before the "weatherman" if something happened in the sky, people took notice. If it rained on a certain day or if an animal acted a certain way, the weather might change. People needed to know when it would rain or snow or when the first frost would come so they could plan their work on the farm.

Chapter 10--Entertainment **151**

  The Pie Supper 152

    Powell, Wayne
    Ava and Eminence, Missouri

    Personal experiences of this writer

  Picnics 156

    Personal experiences of this writer

  Cake Suppers 162

    Personal experiences of this writer

  Play Parties 163

    Personal experiences of this writer

  Music Parties 163

    Personal experiences of this writer

  Songs, Singing and Other Country Music 164

    Personal experiences of this writer

    The songs and fiddle tunes listed were selected because the people made them popular. They played them over and over again. They are still playing and singing the same tunes and songs that they enjoyed many years ago.

  Reading Material 169

    Personal experiences of this writer

    Most families had their own favorite reading material. The following books and newspapers were kept around all the time in our family

      Comfort. Augusta, Maine, W.H. Gannett Co., Vol. XXXII, No. 10, August 1920.

> *Illustrated Companion.* New York, New York, F.B. Warner Co., Vol. 55, No. 9, October 1926. Haines, T.L. and L.W. Yaggy.
>
> *The Royal Path of Life or Aims and Aids for Success and Happiness.* Nashville, Tennessee: Southwestern Publishing Co., 1876.
>
> McGovern, John. *Golden Censer or Duties of Today And Hopes of the Future.* Chicago: Union Pub. Co., 1883.

Tricksters 177

> Decker, E.C. (1895-1990)
> Tecumseh, Missouri
>
> McClendon, Frank
> Gainesville, Missouri
>
> Fraizer, Margaret Evans
> Thornfield, Missouri
>
> Thurman, Jim
> Ava, Missouri
>
> Personal experiences of this writer

Jokes and Short Stories 187
> Many men and women of the Ozarks were good story "tellers". They laughed as they told them and enjoyed the company of others who could tell one they had never heard.

Telephone Entertainment 201
> Personal experiences of this writer

Dancing 205
> McCann, Gordon
> Springfield, Missouri

Personal experiences of this writer

Weddings and Charivaris 208

Personal experiences of this writer

Photography 211

Personal experiences of this writer

Kangaroo Court 213

Personal experiences of this writer

Fun With Anvils, Cotton Rocks and Shotguns 215

Decker, Jonathan (1855-1946)
Birdtown, Missouri

Decker, E.C. (1895-1990)
Tecumseh, Missouri

Memorial Day or Decoration Day 216

Personal experiences of this writer

To Course a Bee 217

Personal experiences of this writer

Chapter 11--Farm Customs 219

Butchering 224

Personal experiences of this writer

Thrashing 226

Martin, Tennessee James (1860-1941)
Dawt, Missouri

Personal experiences of this writer

Molasses Making 228

Personal experiences of this writer

Chapter 12--Church Activities 231

 All-Day-Meeting and Dinner-on-the-Ground 232

  Personal experiences of this writer

 Church Business Meetings 236

  Decker, E.C. (1895-1990)
  Tecumseh, Missouri

  Personal experiences of this writer

 The Church Debate 238

  Decker, E.C. (1895-1990)
  Tecumseh, Missouri

 Baptizings 239

  Decker, Mona Gaulding
  Ava, Missouri

  Personal experiences of this writer

 Protracted Meetings 241

  Personal experiences of this writer

 The Brush Arbor 242

  Personal experiences of this writer

Chapter 13--A Death in the Family 247

 Personal experiences of this writer

Chapter 14--One Room Schools in the Ozarks 253

 Decker, Mona Gaulding
 Ava, Missouri

 Personal experiences of this writer

Chapter 15--Folk History 271

Murders 271

    Decker, Jonathan (1855-1946)
    Birdtown, Missouri

    The mystery of a body found in a pond excited people in a small community, especially if the body was that of a young boy.

Tall Tales 273

    Clem, Donald
    Fairfield Bay, Arkansas

    Decker, Jonathan (1855-1946)
    Birdtown, Missouri

Chapter 16--The Supernatural 281

  Beliefs 282

    Martin, Tennessee James (1860-1941)
    Dawt, Missouri

  Ghost Stories 285

    Decker, E.C. (1895-1900)
    Tecumseh, Missouri

    Decker, Jonathan (1855-1946)
    Birdtown, Missouri

    Lirley, Alice
    Goodhope and Redbank Communities
    Douglas County, Missouri

    Mrs. Lirley collected the following ghost stories for me in October of 1998: "The Haunted House," "The Singing Kettle," "Rappins," "The House Haunted by a Headless Ghost," "Rail Fence Ghost," "The Church Place Ghost," and "The Man-Eating Booger of Booger County."

Mrs. Lirley got the stories from the following people in Douglas and Taney County, Missouri: her step-father Lorie Maggard; her husband Gary Lirley of the Goodhope and Redbank communities in Douglas County, Missouri; Gladys Keen of the Goodhope, Missouri area; her mother Rocca Maggard of Brown Branch, Missouri. Her mother also lived on Brushy Creek near the town of Bradleyville, Missouri in Taney County when she was first married.

Telling Your Fortune 297

>Martin, Tennessee James (1860-1941)
Dawt, Missouri

Marked Babies 298

>Martin, Tennessee James (1860-1941)
Dawt, Missouri

>Personal experiences of this writer

Made in the USA
Coppell, TX
06 December 2021